SKILLS DRILLS AND BELLYACHES

A Cyclocross Primer
As demonstrated by Jeremy Powers,
2012 U.S. Cyclocross National Champion

By Bill Schieken and Dan Tille
Photography by Bruce Buckley
Rusty Williford, Technical Editor
Book Design by Jennifer Franko Dudek

ACKNOWLEDGMENTS
We cannot thank enough the people who generously donated their time to help us make this book possible: Jeremy Powers, Wes Schempf, Chris Mayhew, Larry Miller, Chris Carraway, Paul Rades, Colby Waller, Thori Wolfe, Nicholas Taylor, Pierce Schmerge, Kevin Hays, Chris Rabadi, Shreya Mehta, Sol Schott, Ryan Jenkins, John Verheul, Taylor Jones, Shira Schieken, Alyssa Severn, Ryan Newill, Paul Muller, Randi Brill, Ryan Dudek, Amy Buckley, Kate Leider Tille and Heather McCurdy.

We would also like to thank our families, friends, clients (past and present) as well as past cyclocross clinic participants. Without their support, this book would not be possible.

COVER DESIGN: Steve Fife
BOOK DESIGN: Jennifer Franko Dudek

FOR MORE INFORMATION ABOUT THE AUTHORS VISIT:
www.cxhairs.com (Bill Schieken)

www.fulcrumcoaching.com (Dan Tille and Rusty Williford)

www.brucebuckleyphotography.com

TABLE OF CONTENTS

TABLE OF CONTENTS

I'm proud to know the authors of this book. I've been privileged enough to be able to work with Dan and Bill at our yearly 'cross camps throughout the country. They are true cyclocross guys and you can see that throughout these pages. *Skills Drills and Bellyaches* has been years in the making. It is an incredible addition to the cyclocross community.

Dan's and Bill's hard work and determination to see this project through fully has been tremendous. And the photographs by Bruce Buckley do an amazing job bringing to life each skill discussed. This book is meant to be read, studied and passed on to anyone looking to perfect their skill, but my hope is that it lands in the hands of young up-and-comers and newbies to the sport. Each page was crafted with passion, for you to better understand cyclocross. I hope that you can take this into your hometown and teach the next generation our sport how to do these techniques properly so, as a whole, the sport becomes better understood ... and done with proper technique!

The contents of this book are going to help you improve your cyclocross riding without doing any intervals, without any long rides, and without any rigorous training plans. Nailing these concepts and techniques will be one of many steps in a long journey to becoming a cyclo-boss!

I know that I didn't start up as a cyclocross rider knowing the best way to corner, the best way to dismount or the best way to find my pedals at the start. I needed to start at square one just like everyone else. It's resources like this that really can make the difference. A lot of things in 'cross don't come naturally, and it's always great to learn things from the experts. I know I did my fair share of learning over the years!

We've all done that dismount wrong and wondered if we should go to the hospital to check up on our groins. Most of us have mistimed a set of barriers and cleaned our clocks. Enjoy the many, many years of knowledge, the thoughtful tips and the time-honed techniques throughout this book. I look forward to seeing you guys at a 'cross event soon, using all of the techniques you've learned in these pages! Have fun and be safe!

Jeremy Powers

EASTON

PREFACE

This book teaches the techniques and skills that all racers, from beginner to elite, should learn and apply to become a better cyclocross racer. It covers basics, such as what to wear and how to get back on your bike after carrying it over an obstacle, as well as more nuanced starting techniques and how to mentally prepare for your race. Even if you have years of 'cross racing under your bibshorts, you can always make improvements to your game. What is on the following pages helps show you the way.

Skills, Drills and Bellyaches serves as a solid primer for new racers, as well as a means for experienced riders to hone their craft. If you master the skills and techniques covered here, you can go into the cyclocross season with the same fitness you had last year, yet achieve better results. Every time you dismount from your bike you are either gaining or losing time on your competition. For instance, if you are a habitual stutter-stepper on remounts, this can cost you around one second each time you get back on your bike. If you are on a course that requires three remounts per lap and you do six laps in your race, that's 18 seconds wasted. Let's say you have similar issues on the dismount. Same math, 18 seconds lost. You are now 36 seconds behind a competitor who is equally fit, but gets on and off the bike more proficiently.

For those familiar with professional road racing, this concept is similar to the coaching philosophy of Dave Brailsford, British cycling director and Team Sky general manager. Brailsford's "aggregation of marginal gains" emphasizes improving every facet of what you do by one percent. This strategy takes every part of racing, be it training, nutrition, cornering, running, sprinting or bike handling, and improves each of those areas. Put all of these seemingly small gains together and you will see significant improvements.

The chapters ahead break down the skills and techniques necessary to race cyclocross. After reviewing the proper skills and techniques for the most common obstacles and course conditions you will face, this book takes you through the preparation needed in the days leading up to a race and what to do once you are racing.

- What should you pack, eat and wear?
- How should you warm up and pre-ride the course?
- How can you get a good start and set up for a strong finish?

We explain how to accomplish each of these skills, and provide detailed visual examples to give the words more meaning.

Whether you need to refine a particular skill set or get a pro tip from U.S. Cyclocross Champion Jeremy Powers (referred to as JPow Tips), this book has something for everyone.

FDJ

INTRODUCTION

Dismounts, remounts, carrying, shouldering, riding sand, riding mud, cornering, off-camber turns, starts, race strategy: each of these cyclocross skills carries a price tag, and the currency you pay with is time and energy. If you perform each skill proficiently, you will see your cost savings begin to accumulate. Add up all of the seconds gained, energy saved, and bobbles avoided by improving cyclocross-specific skills, and you can bank on being ahead of where you were last year, or even at the beginning of the season. Couple that with improved fitness and race experience and you will start sniffing out those podium positions and be well on your way to fame and fortune, or at the very least a category upgrade.

Among cycling disciplines, cyclocross is arguably the most dynamic, social, and competitive of the lot. Whether you are fighting for the win or 59th place, the battle for each finishing spot is a race within the race. And these battles are playing out in several places at once within the tape of the race circuit. The person fighting for 43rd place, four minutes off the pace of the leader, battles just as hard as the racer contending for the podium. At its essence, a cyclocross race boils down to trying to catch and beat the group in front of you without allowing the group behind you to catch up. At the end of the race, you shake the sweat- and mud-drenched hands of your battle-mates, start to relive every moment of the race, and try to convince yourself that seven days isn't that long to wait until you can do it again.

If this sounds appealing, you are in luck. Cyclocross arguably has one of the lowest barriers for entry. Beginner-level cyclocross bikes can be some of the least expensive on the market, and you can even use a mountain bike or old commuter bike to give cyclocross a try. While some of the elite racers will have shaved legs and several expensive racing bikes, you are just as welcome to show up on race day with hairy legs, hand-me-down shorts, and a 1980s mountain bike.

Although the barrier to entry in cyclocross is low, after your first few races the inevitable quest for improvement begins. Once you get hooked, you'll undoubtedly start to wonder: How do I get faster? How can I win the battles against other competitors? What can I do to better handle corners, barriers, mud, and everything that makes a 'cross race unique? The good news is that while better equipment can make you a bit faster, the real gains come from improving your skills and riding technique. You don't need to break the bank to see big improvements.

Even the most seasoned 'cross racers are always trying to improve their skills and techniques. It is extraordinarily rare to hear of someone racing the perfect 'cross race. Nowhere is this more apparent than at the highest professional level where a momentary lapse in concentration can easily cost a win or a spot on the podium. Sven Nys, one of the all-time greats, continues to improve his skills. Rather than be satisfied with his successes, Nys spends the off-season not on the road bike but in a forest near Antwerp, Belgium, challenging himself with the most difficult terrain he can find.

Cyclocross is a life-long learning opportunity. It offers a chance to continually improve, giving you the satisfaction of mastering a new skill or technique while still challenging you to improve in other areas. And when you are in the heat of the battle, all of the lessons you have learned and skills you have worked hard to master will provide that advantage over your competitors.

And on that final lap—the Laatste Ronde—no matter where you are in the race, the mastered techniques and tactics will help give you that edge on those less prepared. Unlike a road race or criterium in which riders not in contention for a high finishing position often roll across the line in a bunch, a cyclocross racer fights to the end for every position. If you were 36th last week, you want to be at least 35th this week. From first place to 125th, the battle rages fast and fierce. It's all about getting out there and doing it. No matter what your experience or skill level, it's about testing yourself against the course and the competition. It's about the battle.

PART 1

SKILLS

THE START

The start of a cyclocross race is arguably the most important part of the race. Unlike road racing in which the sprint comes at the end of the race, in cyclocross, the field sprint is at the start. Knowing how to efficiently and effectively start gives you a better opportunity to be near the front of the race at the finish. Learning the correct way to start a race not only prevents you from losing time, but also keeps you from expending extra energy unnecessarily. By no means will you win the race by having a good start, but if you do not have the proper skills and know-how, you can most definitely lose the race.

Start Technique

If the start is on a gravel road, lift your rear wheel, get a good pedal stroke to spin the rear tire, then set the bike down to dig out the top level of loose gravel to set the tire for the start. Also clear out the gravel with your unclipped foot so there is no debris under the shoe. If you have a choice where to stage yourself

After you are staged, check your cleats and pedals to ensure that they are free of debris.

on the row, take into consideration where your rear tire will get the most traction, who the rider is (if anyone) in front of you, and if there's a side of the course you'll want to be on immediately after starting.

JPOW TIP If you have pedals with a platform, reach down to the pedal that is not clipped in and level it with the ground so that when you go to clip in, the pedal body is exactly where you want it to be and you are not fumbling around with your free foot trying to clip in (image 1).

For the start, clip in to your pedal with your preferred leg. If you don't know which leg that is, think about when you unclip your shoe to stop at a traffic light or to stop and take a drink. The foot that touches down for stability is your support leg; the leg that remains clipped into the pedal is your preferred leg.

Your cranks should be positioned with the clipped in pedal between the 9 and 10 o'clock position.

JPOW TIP For most racers, starting from the 9 o'clock position helps them get off the line faster than starting from 11 o'clock or higher (image 2).

There are two common start positions. It's a good idea to practice both so that you know which works best for you.

For both options, the most common hand position for the start is on the hoods (image 3).

The first option is to stand over your toptube with one foot clipped in and the other on the ground with your hands on the hoods. The benefit of this option is that it allows your first pedal stroke to be as powerful as possible, however it means that your initial clip in of your stabilizing leg might take a few more pedal strokes. There is also a pause for most people, where their stabilizing leg "finds" the pedal using this technique.

The second option is to be sitting on the saddle with one foot clipped in and the other foot on the ground (for most people this will mean that you are stabilizing yourself on your toe). Your hands are on the hoods. The advantage to this option is you are likely to clip in your stabilizing leg immediately, and allow your subsequent pedal strokes to be more powerful. The drawback to this method is that your initial pedal stroke may not be as explosive as the previous option.

If you are tall enough to do so, i.e., you can reach the ground with your toe while seated, the best option is to try and start sitting on the saddle. By starting on the saddle you will almost always hit the pedal and be off the line and moving, even if you don't immediately clip in. For shorter or less experienced riders, starting while sitting on the saddle may not be an option if you are unable to balance on one toe to stabilize yourself in the starting grid. Among top professionals, few riders start off the saddle.

HOODS VS. DROPS

We just discussed the pros and cons of seating position at the start line. There is also a choice to be made regarding initial hand position—do you place your hands on the brake hoods, or in the drops?

HOODS:

- **PRO:** Starting on the hoods adds more stability when getting off the line, and it also puts your weight just a little bit further back which helps the rear wheel stay planted on the ground and not skipping or spinning out.
- **PRO:** Starting on the hoods puts you in a more natural, stable position to get clipped in.
- **CON:** You are more upright and present a slightly larger cross-section to the wind, so it's less aerodynamic.

DROPS:

- **PRO:** Starting in the drops puts you in the position most racers sprint in when on the road, so power generation is solid and you have the slight aerodynamic advantage (although it is limited since you are starting from a standstill).
- **CON:** Your weight is further forward, sometimes to the point that a substantial fraction of your weight is on the front wheel, which makes you less stable and puts you at risk of your rear tire slipping, or worse, pulling out of a pedal and going over the bars.

When the whistle blows you want to drive down your clipped in pedal and quickly hit the other pedal with your other shoe.

If you do not cleanly clip in the first time your shoe hits the pedal, don't worry about it. It's more important to continue pedaling hard than fussing with your pedal. Once you have established your position in the race, you can worry about properly engaging the cleat.

As stated previously, in cyclocross, as opposed to road racing, the mass sprint happens at the beginning of the race, not at the end. It is important that you get off the line fast and smoothly. Work to get on top of, or spin up, your chosen gear as fast as possible. Once you begin to spin out (you can't pedal any faster), shift 1 or 2 gears—to a smaller cog, or a "bigger" gear—while slightly easing the pedal pressure, then get on top of the next gear. Briefly easing the pressure on the pedals helps reduce the chance of breaking your chain due to shifting under a tremendous load. Also, jumping two gears per shift helps increase the interval between shifts without becoming over-geared during the start. Your main objective is to go fast enough without outsprinting, or overtaxing, yourself. In other words, don't go so hard that you can't recover from these initial efforts, and you quickly give back any gains you made in the start of the race as a result of exhaustion before the race intensity ramps up. The first couple minutes of a race are brutally hard and fast so burn your matches wisely.

MATCHES

A common phrase in bike racing is "burning a match." Think about starting your race with a full book of matches. Every time you make a hard effort, you burn one of those matches. The goal is to make sure you still have that final match left to use at the end of the race. This means you have to be smart in picking the right spots to burn those matches. But it also means not finishing the race with several matches leftover. In other words, use them wisely but make sure you use them.

That being said, the start of the race hurts. It's all part of the game. You need to go a little into the red to make sure you put yourself into a good position entering the first set of features. The goal is to make sure you are in the right group, and that you arrive there without using unnecessary energy, crashing or being impeded by slower riders. Winning the start is less important than not messing up the start. Finally, the start is often the most hectic, crowded moment of the race. The basic motions of getting off the line and getting up to speed need to be so well-practiced that they are intuitive. Focus your attention on not running into the riders in front of you and make enough space for yourself in the scrum of sprinting riders.

START GEARING

The appropriate starting gear depends on your power output and the starting conditions. You want to pick a gear that will allow you to accelerate quickly. A good rule of thumb is to choose a gear that you can get on top of (i.e. spin up) within the first 3-5 seconds of the race. You don't want to be over-geared, as the key is to get off the line as quickly as possible, then shift into harder gears as you accelerate. For a flat, paved start a good choice could be the big front chainring, and your largest or second largest cog in the back, whereas an uphill grass start may necessitate using the small front chainring.

Powers, who can generate a ton of power quickly, starts in his small ring and a large cog on the cassette (38x23). Powers is more comfortable spinning at an extremely high rate than mashing a bigger gear, and he finds himself at the front of most every race he starts.

START DRILLS

The following exercises are designed to help practice starts and determine which gearing works best. These drills will allow you to try out various starting techniques, hand positions and gear ratios prior to race day.

(1) With a group, line up two rows deep on a 1/8 to 1/4 mile stretch of road or flat ground. For example, if you have eight people, line-up in rows of four. Assign one person with the job of starter. That person will announce to the group that there are 15 seconds to go before the start. At any time during the next 15 seconds, the starter will yell, "Go!" (This element of surprise accurately reenacts the race official blowing the whistle. You never quite know when this will happen after the official announces 30 seconds to go.) When that happens, go. Set up maybe one obstacle or off-camber turn after the starting stretch so that you're racing hard for around 30 seconds to a minute, but still need to negotiate a semi-tricky obstacle after 30-60 seconds of going all out. This drives home not only the mechanics of getting off the line quickly, and dealing with traffic, but you get used to having to settle down and negotiate something tricky right afterwards – just like a race. Repeat the drill with a new starter. The drill can be done with as few as two people or even solo, but is more effective if you have at least one other person to share the starter job.

(2) Using the format of the drill above, switch up how you start. Start standing up, sitting down, in a bigger gear, in an easier gear, etc. Also do a couple starts in which you purposefully do not clip in cleanly. Practice being able to accelerate without your pedal engaged.

(3) If you have a midweek 'cross practice that does circuits on a course, break up the session into at least 2 or 3 separate intervals, and do a real group start before each interval. If you're a fast local rider who struggles with 4th and 5th row starting spots when you go to big races, then start at the back and get used to picking your way through people.

DISMOUNT FOR STANDARD CARRY

The primary difference between cyclocross and other disciplines of bike racing is that at some point during the race you are going to have to get off of your bike. Learning to dismount your bike smoothly and efficiently allows you to keep momentum through the transition. 'Cross is all about maintaining momentum. If you need to scrub speed to dismount your bike, you lose momentum, which translates to time and energy wasted. Having proper technique allows you to dismount faster and more efficiently, which conserves your momentum. As a result, you are faster while expending less energy.

The dismount is a skill you will want to practice above all others before entering your first race. If you've never practiced getting off of a moving bike before trying to do so in a race, you will most likely approach the obstacle either too tentatively, which will cost you time, or you will approach too fast and run the risk of crashing into the barrier. Unless you are seeking instant Internet notoriety and possible injury, practice the dismount before you race.

JPOW TIP Before you begin dismounting your bike, make sure you are prepared for the remount. This means knowing the terrain on the other side of the obstacle and the correct gearing for the remount. Make sure you are in the correct gear when you dismount so that it's easy to start pedaling again once you get back on. Remember, it's all about conserving and maintaining momentum. Pick the wrong gear for the remount, and you will lose momentum.

Gear selection for the remount is an instance in which the pre-ride lap, which is discussed later in this book, is important. When you are doing your pre-race laps, figure out the optimal gear to be in for all remounts so that you will have this information dialed-in by the time the race starts.

To properly dismount the bike, place both hands on the hoods and regulate your speed (i.e., feather the brakes to reach the speed you can safely dismount for the obstacle). As you get more proficient you will be able to approach barriers faster, but the last thing you want to do is to suddenly decelerate or stop before dismounting. It's better to approach the obstacle a little too slowly and maintain your speed throughout the dismount than to come in too fast and have to brake hard.

BRAKE SETUP

On a bike that is set up conventionally, pulling the left-hand brake lever will slow the front wheel rather than the rear and could cause you to topple over the front of the bike. To avoid this happening, some racers reverse the brakes on their cyclocross bikes so that the left hand controls the rear brake and the right hand controls the front brake. You may consider doing this on all your bikes for consistency, should you prefer your levers "switched" for 'cross.

After placing your hands on the hoods, you are going to unclip but not remove your left shoe from the pedal. Instead, place the center of your shoe on the center of the pedal body (image 1). Because many shoes have different tread patterns it may take some trial and error to find that sweet spot in which your shoe is stable on the pedal. This may be a bit difficult if you have carbon-soled shoes. An easy trick is to cut out part of an old bike tire and glue it to the smooth center section of your shoe.

Unclipping the left foot early and well in advance of an obstacle is the safest technique and a good idea for all beginners. It is known as "pre-unclipping." Once you are more proficient in dismounting the bike you may opt to stay clipped in longer. Many veteran cyclocross racers do not unclip their left shoe until just before they place that foot on the ground. The risk of doing so is that you won't be able to unclip in time or your pedal refuses to release the shoe and is stuck. If this happens, the chances the rider will crash—or at the very least lose some of that valuable momentum—are high. By pre-unclipping you give yourself a safety net. By leaving plenty of room to ensure that the shoe is properly unclipped, your chances of crashing diminish greatly.

After the left shoe is unclipped and resting on the pedal, unclip the right shoe from its pedal (image 2).

Once the right shoe is unclipped, lift your right leg over the saddle and rear wheel while maintaining your balance on the left pedal. Both hands are still on the hoods and you are maintaining forward momentum as you roll toward the obstacle (image 3).

Once your right leg is on the dismount side of the bike and behind the left leg, there are two techniques commonly used to get your right foot on the ground. You can either step your right foot between the frame and your left leg, called the step-through, or you can place your right leg down behind your left leg, known as the step-behind.

The step-through method, in which the right foot travels between the left leg and the bike frame, is a more difficult maneuver that carries with it a higher risk and consequence of failure. When doing the step-through your hips are rotating counter-clockwise to keep your right foot in line and your body straight. At the same time, your left leg must rotate the opposite way to leave the pedal and make contact with the ground. Having your body going two directions at once is a risky proposition especially when you are tired and oxygen-depleted at the end of a race. While advocates of the step-through claim it is faster for high speed barrier sections, in practice riders lose no time stepping behind. As such, it appears to be more of a style recommendation.

We recommend using the step-behind method because there is a much higher risk of crashing if the left foot does not unclip while stepping through as opposed to stepping behind. Also, stepping behind is faster for sections where you want to pedal for as long as possible before dismounting. For example, the middle of a half-rideable sandpit, or halfway up a steep, half-rideable hill.

To perform the step-behind technique, your right foot, after swinging over the saddle and rear wheel, comes to rest behind and to the outside of your left foot (see image 1, opposite). Your foot is not touching the ground but hovering a couple inches above it. Your right hip should be pressed firmly into the side of the saddle, or for some, the nose of the saddle; this allows you to control the bike once you remove one of your hands (image 2). While the right foot is coming to rest behind the left foot, your right hand should move from the right shifter hood to the toptube. The right hand grabs the toptube at the balance point, usually just in front of the nose of the saddle, of your bike. Proper placement of the hand on the toptube ensures you lift the bike with your elbow between you and the bike.

At this point, you should still have forward momentum rolling the bike towards the obstacle.

JPOW TIP Place the palm of your right hand flat on top of the toptube, with a 90-degree bend in the wrist. If you place your hand without the 90-degree bend, you will be much more likely to lift the bike with your elbow on the outside of the saddle, thereby jamming the saddle under your armpit.

Coasting on the bike while standing on a pedal with your right hand on the toptube takes some getting used to. This is the transitional phase between riding and running. To ensure that you are stable and balanced, concentrate on maintaining three points of contact between you and your bike:

- Right hand on toptube/hip on saddle, with the right forearm between the nose of the saddle and your body
- Left hand on left shifter hood
- Unclipped left shoe on left pedal

When you are ready to complete the dismount, your right foot should touch the ground first (image 3). As soon as the right foot touches the ground, the left foot should follow. Your forward momentum will dictate that you hit the ground running. Some people will feel they need a bit of a jump off of the left pedal with the left foot, to be sure they are not still clipped in. As you begin to run, your right hand maintains its position at the balance point on the toptube and your left hand stays on the hoods. This is a basic starting point for carrying the bicycle.

When dismounting the bike, you want to leave enough room between you and the quickly approaching barrier. A good rule of thumb is to give yourself at least two or three full running strides off the bike before reaching the first barrier. As you become more proficient, like Jeremy in the photos, you may be able to shorten the distance, but two to three strides is a good starting point.

BALANCE POINT

To find the balance point, lift your bike from the ground with your right hand on the toptube. Your right hand should act as the fulcrum. Find the point on the toptube in which the bike levels out when lifted off the ground. This is the balance point, where your right hand should be placed during dismounting and preparing to carry the bike over the barriers. If you grab the toptube too close to the head tube the rear wheel will be lower. If you grab it too close to the seatpost, the front wheel will be lower, the balance point is where the wheels are level.

1.

fi'zi:k
2.

fi'zi:k
3.

JPOW TIP

When you become more proficient at dismounting, you will notice that your right pedal body will come to rest near the top of the pedal stroke. As you increase the speed of the dismount, the pedal body should progress slightly so it is approximately ¾ around the pedal stroke. If this does not naturally occur for you (somewhat common if you pre-unclip) then add in a slight ankle flick of your left foot as it leaves the pedal body. This will move the pedal body to the desired remount location, at about the 2 o'clock position.

Standard Carry

After you have dismounted, it is time to either carry or shoulder the bike. The standard carry, which we will discuss first, is used mainly for barriers and to cover short distances off the bike.

After you dismount and begin to run, it is time to lift the bike off the ground. Your right hand is already on the toptube at the balance point and your left hand is on the shifter hood. (See photos on page 13.)

When lifting your bike make sure to lift it high enough off the ground to clear the obstacle and keep the wheels level. How high you need to lift the bike will change depending on the barrier, but around knee high is a good starting point. For example, if you are carrying the bike over a set of barriers (also called planks) you need to have the bike high enough so that the tires do not hit the top of the obstacle. (See photos on page 14.)

When carrying the bike, your right arm should be partially extended so that the right elbow is between your body and the frame. Avoid having the bike up against your body and do not tuck the saddle into your armpit. This technique serves several functions. First, the bike is easier to control if you accidentally carry it too low and hit the barrier. Instead of the bike saddle shooting upward into your armpit, it is away from the body and less likely to cause a crash. Second, it prevents the bike from becoming tangled in your legs as you run. Third, it creates space and makes it more difficult for a competitor to pass you while running the barriers. Fourth, especially for

Rapha
FOCUS

Rapha
FOCUS

Rapha
FOCUS
EASTON

Rapha
FOCUS
EASTON

Rapha
FOCUS
fi'zi:k

Rapha

shorter riders or uphill (effectively higher) barriers, it allows you to lift the bike higher to clear the barriers. Without a doubt, there are many accomplished racers and even top level pros who carry their bike with the saddle in their armpit. That does not mean, however, it is the safest and most efficient technique.

An alternative method for carrying the bicycle over barriers is to lift from the downtube rather than the toptube. This is a preferred method for shorter riders and is also a popular method used to shoulder the bike. To carry from the downtube:

- Keep your right hand on the hood, unclip your left foot from the pedal and leave it there.
- Bring your right leg over the saddle and rear wheel following the same setup procedure discussed above.
- Move the right hand from the hood to roughly the middle of the downtube.
- Bring your right foot to the ground, followed by the left. You will use the same step-behind technique discussed above.
- While running, pull up on the downtube with your right hand. The outside of your right forearm, near the elbow, will make contact with the toptube (see image 1 and 2, page 16).
- Lift up the bike over the barriers. Note that the bike is able to be lifted higher while the arm remains relatively low (see image 3, page 16) and that the bike remains level throughout the carry (see image 4, page 16).

An optional technique is to move the right hand from the hood to the balance point on the toptube and then to the downtube. This technique adds an extra step but may add to stability when coasting before the carry.

The advantage of this carry is that lifting from the downtube allows the shorter rider to easily raise the bike higher off the ground, ensures there is enough clearance to get over the barrier without knocking the bike into it, and requires less upper-body effort to raise the bike higher than the standard carry. The downtube-grab is not only used by shorter riders over barriers, it's also used by most riders for shouldering (as you will see later). What becomes obvious is that, if you must have a water-bottle cage on your bike (either for training or for very hot races), you want it on the seat tube–not the downtube. It's nearly impossible to execute a smooth downtube grab with a waterbottle cage right where you want your hand to go.

Riding Barriers

A skill new racers are always curious about is the ability to ride over the barriers instead of having to dismount the bike. This technique is sometimes referred to as hopping the barriers. However, a hop technically involves jumping your bike over an obstacle without the tires touching the obstacle. Some racers have mastered this skill and it is usually performed on high-speed barriers. It is a technique that carries a lot of risk.

Hopping is not what most cyclocross racers do when they ride barriers. Instead of hopping over, the conventional technique is to lift the front tire on to the top of the barrier and while pedaling then lift the back end of the bike over. This is a difficult skill that takes years to master. It is also one that we are not going to cover in this book.

This is a skill that could save you a second or two each lap. However, it is also a technique that can cost you minutes or even the whole race, if you mess up the timing and crash your bike.

Only ride the barriers if you are 100 percent confident you can successfully do it 100 percent of the time. At the end of the race, when you are tired and not thinking straight is when trying to do something tricky like riding a barrier could go wrong.

DISMOUNT DRILL

A good drill to practice for becoming comfortable with dismounts is to find a flat grass field and start pedaling at a moderate pace. Unclip your left shoe and keep it on the pedal. Unclip your right foot and swing the right leg over the toptube and behind the left shoe, setting up for the step-behind. For the first several times through the drill keep both hands on the hoods and coast as far as you can, concentrating on the three points of contact (hand on hood, hip and thigh against bike, foot on pedal). When the bike begins to lose momentum, dismount. After you have run through the drill in a straight line, do it again, but when you begin to coast, turn the bike left. Once comfortable with that, turn the bike to the right while coasting. This is a bit harder because you are balancing your body on the left side of the bike and will need to lean into it to turn right. When that skill has been mastered, do the drill again and this time remove the right hand from the hood and grab the toptube while continuing to coast.

Once you are comfortable, place three or four cones in a straight line with about 20 feet of space between the cones. Repeat the drill and practice slaloming between the cones. This will force you to steer your bike with one hand on the shifter hood and one hand on the toptube. The drill gives you an appreciation for balancing and steering your bike from the dismount position.

KICK DRILL

To become even more familiar with the three points of contact position, you can extend the previous drill. Once your right leg is stacked on the left side with your hip planted solidly against the saddle, you can sustain your momentum by using your right leg to propel you forward, like kicking on a skateboard. This drill allows you to spend more time handling the bike with your legs stacked on the left and adds the dynamic kicking action to the mix, which helps you get more comfortable encountering momentum changes as well as directional changes in this position.

Rapha

REMOUNT

Once you have cleared the barriers, you will most likely be breathing hard and your legs will feel like they are on fire. For most cyclists, running is the last thing we want to do and our body lets us know as much every time our feet hit the ground. There is no greater instinct after clearing a set of barriers than wanting to drop the bike and jump back on. But as easy and appealing as that sounds, it can result in disaster and should be avoided.

The first step in the remount is to gently set your bike on the ground while continuing to run forward. This is done in a smooth, fluid motion.

The rookie mistake is to unceremoniously drop the bike on the ground. The drop and flop will cause a couple of problems that will slow you down or completely stop you. Dropping the bike may cause your chain to drop off of the chainrings. At the very least, this will cause you to lose momentum as you reach down to try and readjust the chain. It may also force you to stop and fix the problem. Dropping the bike will also cause the back end of the bike to bounce around, making your remount difficult because the saddle will bounce up and down rather than remaining level.

The bike should be set on the ground so gently that the chain does not bounce (image 1).

After you have set the bike down you may have to run with the bike for several feet to settle the bike and properly set yourself up for a good remount (image 2).

Once the bike is settled and your hands have returned to the hoods, the remount starts with a slight opening up of the hips toward the bike (image 3). Your right leg (for standard left-side dismount/remount) will be led by a high-knee. This opening of the hips and high-knee drive allows your thigh to clear the back of your saddle (image 4). During a

full-speed remount, at this phase your right thigh should be parallel with the ground and starting to sweep forward to contact the saddle. Envision the trail leg of a track hurdler here. The aim is for your inner right thigh to make contact with the saddle (image 5 and 6). The purpose of this, for men and women, should be obvious, but it also provides a stable platform with lots of muscular padding for you to use. Initially, you may want to have your target area an inch or two south of the chamois stitching; as you get more experienced, this target landing area will move to approximately right on the chamois stitching (image 7 and 8).

As soon as you have made contact with the saddle, naturally rotate your right leg in a pedaling motion such that the right foot contacts the right pedal (image 1 and 2). Getting your foot rapidly onto the pedal should be the goal of every remount, as it conserves momentum. At this point you should put pressure on the pedal and your hips will naturally rotate such that you slide gently on to the saddle and your body is centered. Continue to apply pressure to the pedal on the down-stroke, don't worry about clipping back in at this point (image 3 and 4). The reason for this is simple; as we have stated repeatedly, a primary goal in cyclocross is to maintain momentum, and getting a down stroke into the right pedal during the

1.

2.

remount will ensure you maintain your forward momentum. At t
your left foot will begin to naturally follow the pedal stroke path and
likely find the pedal body. As you continue to apply pedal force, begin
process of clipping back into the pedals.

If you are carrying the bike from the downtube, bend your knees to settle the bike on the ground and move your right hand from the downtube to the right hood/bars (images 1 and 2).

After both hands are back on the bars, move your right leg over the saddle, almost like you are stepping over a large obstacle.

CHAINKEEPER

One way to help prevent your chain from dropping is to use a chainwatcher or chainkeeper that attaches to your seat tube and helps keep the chain on the rings. However, these devices are not foolproof, and if the chain comes off while using one, it will most likely lodge itself between the device and the chainring and you may need a multi-tool to loosen the guard and reset the chain. Even if you don't have a helper, wheels or a bike in the pit area, bring a small tool roll (or even just a multi-tool) and place it in the pit for your race. This way, if you have any sort of mechanical you can run your bike to the pit and try to fix the issue instead of dropping out of the race. You should also be sure to run your chain at the correct length. Many bikes are set up with the chain length too long.

s not going to be in the ideal position, but rd momentum so you want to be pedaling ped in. Because you already thought about pe in before you dismounted, you are ready

e have is the double- or stutter-step, which ittle hop, skip and a jump routine before remounting. This is another time-waster that, when eliminated, will save you seconds during every lap. To break the habit you have to slow the process down and take it one step at a time. See the drill at right for how to do this.

Another bad habit people develop is the "Superman" remount. Instead of sliding onto the saddle, the rider jumps off the ground as if they are going to leap tall buildings in a single bound!

Jumping on to your saddle is not only inefficient but can lead to disaster. First, you could pinch-flat a tire, second, you could break or bend your seat or seatpost, and third, you can break yourself. Gentlemen, that means you. The superman technique results in the rider not engaging the pedals as quickly, and a delay in getting back up to speed. If the rider next to you engages the pedals before you, that's a few extra feet advantage every remount.

SUPERMAN

REMOUNT DRILL

In an open field, walk next to your bike and slowly practice lifting your right leg, stepping over the seat, and landing on your right thigh. Initially this works best when performed on a slight downhill, so you don't have to struggle with keeping your forward momentum. Don't worry about the drive through to the pedal at this point. Just land on your right thigh and coast for a couple of feet, then start over again. As you become more comfortable with opening your hips, driving a high knee and sweeping over the saddle, you will start finding the pedal body more easily. Practice your dismount technique and reset yourself. There is no need to rush in this drill. Take it as slowly as you need to ensure you have perfect technique. You are going to be that crazy guy at the public park getting on and off of a perfectly functional bicycle, but repetition is key. Not just 10, 20, or hundreds of times, but thousands of times. Practice makes perfect, the devil is in the details, a stitch in time, whatever cliché works best for you, embrace it and practice, practice, practice. Practicing at a walking pace means you can do it safely almost anywhere, and has the added benefit of forcing you to focus on balance as well as the skill.

Once you have the move down and have eliminated any semblance of a stutter-step, increase the speed. You may notice during a brisk walking remount that it helps if you push off a bit more forcefully with your left foot as your right leg drives up. Once you have mastered the fast walking step-over, move on to a slow jog. This is the point in which most people develop the stutter-step, because they believe that as they remount they are going to land square on their tender bits. If you start stutter-stepping again, slow back down a notch. One helpful tip is to jog with a bit more of a bounce in your step, actively using your hands on the hoods to support your body weight. Then with the bouncing jog, remount. Stay at this point for a considerable time to imprint the muscle memory. Finally, move to a more fluid jog or run and remount. Again, if a stutter-step arises, back up to the last speed you did in which you did not stutter-step. Focusing on springing up and forward off the left toe is another good visual that helps eliminate the stutter-step. You can't stutter-step if you've committed to the remount with the left leg. Continue the drill until you can smoothly remount at full speed.

Putting It All Together

Through a barrier section, the dismount, carry and remount should be a smooth, continuous motion. When mastered you will carry speed through the run and remount with momentum. At the pro level, riders take the barriers as a natural part of the course and get off and back on to the bike with an insignificant change in speed.

You'll notice that as the barriers are cleared, it is not a jump, but rather a smooth stride with a high leading knee. Many inexperienced riders find themselves leaping like a gazelle over the planks, which is slower and a waste of energy. Also, some riders find that they can only clear the planks when leading with a certain leg, which causes them to stutter-step as they approach the barriers. If you find yourself doing either, or both, of these through the planks, there are some easy drills to help speed you up.

Note the high leading knee and smoothness of motion in the remount sequence on pages 25, 26 and 27.

Rapha
FOCUS

Rapha
FOCUS

Rapha
FOCUS

Rapha
FOCUS

FOCUS

BARRIER DRILL

Set up a pair of barriers, you can build your own out of PVC piping, or even find a log, and set your bike to the side. It may feel odd at first, but run the barriers without your bike while concentrating on leading with a high knee, but not leaping over the feature. To allow your back foot to clear the feature, think of doing a butt-kicker. Strive to be as smooth as possible, keeping your head and body from bouncing high over the barrier. Next, do the drill while leading with your other leg. Focus even more time on this leg, as you want to be as comfortable leading with your non-dominant leg as you are with your dominant leg. Next, do the drill with your dominant leg leading the first barrier, and your non-dominant leg leading over the second barrier. Continue to do these running drills until clearing the barriers with either leg feels smooth and natural. Now pick up your bike and repeat the drills, not worrying about dismounting or remounting, just running the planks with the bike, while focusing on smooth, fluid motions.

Rapha.
FOCUS

Rapha.
FOCUS

CARRYING AND SHOULDERING

If an obstacle is too slippery or steep to ride and too long to efficiently run using the standard carry, it is often best to shoulder the bike. Shouldering takes a little longer to set up, but you can cover longer distances faster using this method.

As you approach the obstacle but before dismounting, make sure you are in an appropriate gear for your remount. Finding which gear is appropriate is something you should address during your warm up laps. Experiment with different gearing options pre-race. Dismount using similar technique as the standard dismount, placing the right hand on the toptube or downtube. Maintain the three points of contact: right hand on toptube/hip on saddle, with the right forearm between the nose of the saddle and your body, left hand on left shifter hood, and unclipped left shoe on left pedal.

You can lift the bike in two primary ways, by the toptube or by the downtube. Generally, when shouldering on flat ground at higher speed, the toptube lift is most natural and is often the easiest for riders with longer arms as the forearm/ elbow fit through the frame triangle easier using a toptube lift. The downtube lift becomes a smoother option when shouldering on an incline or at slower speed, although some find that the elbow hits the seat-tube on smaller frames. Practice both techniques to see which works best for you.

Toptube Lift

To lift by the toptube, start with your hand in the standard dismount position, grasping the toptube with your knuckles on top (image 1).

As your left foot strikes the ground, flip your right hand and grab the toptube by the underside (knuckles on bottom). This allows you to hoist the bike to your shoulder (image 2).

Lift the bike up and onto your shoulder using your bicep as your elbow slides inside the frame triangle (image 3). The weight will transfer from your palm to your thumb as this rotation progresses (image 4).

Place the toptube onto your shoulder; don't drop the bike (image 5). Then release your right hand and move your right arm to complete the arm wrap (discussed later) (image 6).

Downtube Lift

To lift the bike using the downtube, prepare just as you would for a standard dismount, except keep your right arm between your body and the bike. Open the right hand and reach straight down to grab the downtube. The point at which you grab the downtube depends on the balance-point of your bike (see page 10), and the length of your forearm compared to the geometry of your frame triangle. Ideally, you will grab the downtube where the bike is in perfect balance with just your right hand holding it; sometimes this point is closer toward the bottom bracket, causing your elbow to hit the seat-tube when lifting. Find this ideal lifting point when you are standing stationary next to your bike. When learning this skill for the first time, some like to put a piece of black electrical tape at the grab spot to help guide their hand placement. After a little practice, it becomes muscle memory to grab in the correct location.

As you begin the lift, initially your back will be slightly bent at the waist and your right arm will be fully extended (image 1). Begin to straighten your back and use the strength in your legs and arms to lift the bike upward (image 2). Note that the forearm is also used to help stabilize the bike during the lift, and for some with less hand/wrist strength, this can become a greater asset in the lift (image 3).

As the bike begins to fully lift, your elbow will slot into the frame triangle and the toptube will naturally start to slide up to the shoulder (images 1 and 2, page 32). Again, place the bike gently onto the shoulder and release your right hand so your right arm can perform the arm wrap (images 3 and 4, page 32).

As your right hand grabs the bars, your left hand releases and is slightly bent at your left side in a running position. When running, keep the body upright and loose. Keep your head up to see where you are going.

Arm Wrap

Once the bike is on your shoulder—either via the toptube lift—or the downtube lift, your right arm will wrap around the outside of the frame to further provide stability. There are generally three types of arm wraps used: headtube wrap, downtube wrap, and the "bro" wrap, which is not recommended.

1.
2.
3.
4.

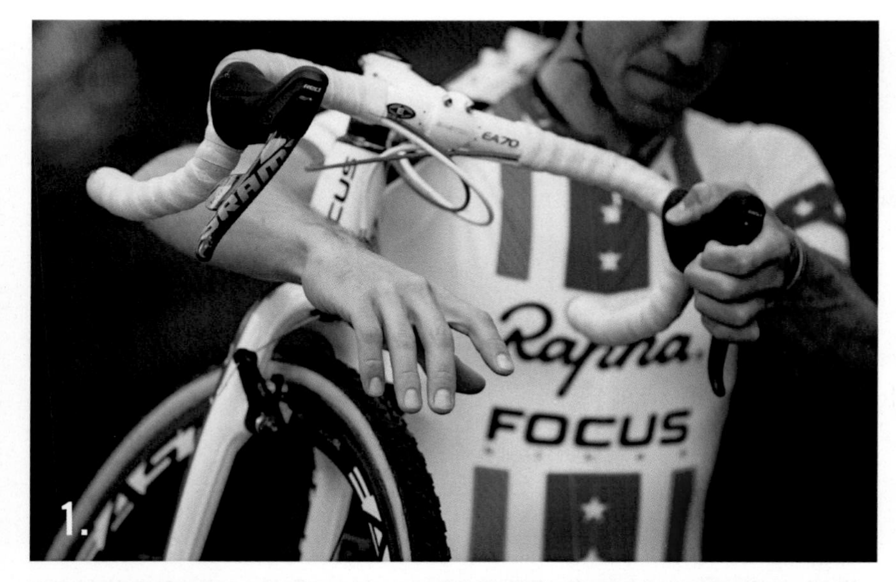

Headtube Wrap

For riders with longer arms—and many of the elite men—the headtube wrap is preferred. It allows riders who can perform it to carry the bike in a more parallel way, such that the weight of the toptube is distributed more evenly across the back and both shoulders. The nose of the saddle tends to be farther away from the back of your helmet with this carry, which means it can't hit your head or move your helmet.

To perform the headtube wrap, bring your right arm around the outside of the headtube, just under the handlebars (image 1). Reach through with your right arm and grasp the hood of the left shifter, where your left hand is currently holding. Once the left hand transfers the shifter hood to the right hand, release the left hand and use your right hand to gently pull the bike slightly in and parallel across your back (image 2). Pulling the bike in slightly moves the saddle away from the back of your helmet, and allows you to stand upright instead of running hunched over. The type of front brake you use, and the routing of cables in front of the headtube on your bike may make the headtube wrap difficult.

With the bike securely on your back, stabilized by your right arm wrapped around the headtube, you can run naturally upright. Use your left arm as a counter-balance or to protect you from an errant bike swung wildly by your less skilled competition.

Downtube Wrap

An alternate technique is the downtube wrap. It is preferred by riders with shorter arms and by some who find it more comfortable and controllable. Some with less upper body strength find that the downtube wrap allows them to relieve some of the pressure on their shoulders by using their right forearm and hand to slightly lift the bike.

To execute the downtube wrap, bring your right arm around the outside of the downtube and under it. To make this arm movement safer—avoiding the spinning front wheel—use your left hand to turn the handlebars slightly to the left, opening the area under the downtube (images 1-3).

After the arm clears the downtube and tire, reach for the left drop of your handlebar and grasp it with your right hand (images 4 and 5).

Release your left hand and use your right arm to pull the handlebar—and the bike—toward your chest (image 6). This moves the saddle away from your helmet and allows you to open your shoulders a bit to distribute the weight across more of your back, instead of solely on your right shoulder.

Again, stand upright so that your running motion is more natural and allow your left arm to swing naturally. If you wish to relieve some of the pressure of the bike on your shoulders, squeeze the downtube between your bicep and forearm—inside of your forearm—insideand lift your arm up. This stabilizes the bike and allows you to bear some of the bike's weight on your arm.

Proper Shouldering

When the bike is properly shouldered you have three points of contact: the right hand on left hood (for headtube wrap) or the left handlebar drop (for downtube wrap); the crook of elbow on downtube or headtube; and the toptube on the right shoulder and back (image 1). When these three points of contact are established, both you and your bike are stable. If you get bumped or are going up a steep hill, you are moving as one with the bike instead of fighting it. Also, your left arm is free to assist with more effective running and to catch yourself if you happen to slip up a steep, slippery hill (image 2).

JPOW TIP As you begin to run, reach behind you with your left hand and line up the left crank arm with the chainstay. This allows for the pedals to be in the ideal spot for the remount. This subtle move will save your back from getting a pedal body rammed into it while running (image 3).

Bro-Wrap

A third technique—one that is not recommended—is to place your right hand over the toptube and on, or over, the right tops of the handlebar. This is sometimes referred to as the "bro" method, as it looks like a rider is putting his arm around his bro. It is not recommended because the bike is not as stable, your body is not in an optimal position to run, the majority of the bike's weight is borne on your right shoulder, the saddle has a greater chance of hitting the back of your head, and getting your hands back into position for the remount is more difficult.

Although the "bro-wrap," which is also known as "Swiss style," is not recommended, it is better than the "javelin" method in which the bike is on the shoulder, the right hand holds the toptube and the bars swing freely.

Un-Shouldering

When you have cleared the obstacle and are ready to remount the bike, bring your left hand up to the left shifter hood. This provides stability as you let go of the handlebar with your right hand. Unwrap your right arm from around the headtube or downtube and allow the bike to slide forward on your shoulder.

Just as with the lift to carry, there are also two techniques to bring the bike off of your shoulder: toptube transfer and downtube transfer. For the toptube transfer, reach your right hand up and hook your right thumb under the toptube to lift the bike off your shoulder. Unfold your right arm through the frame triangle and gently set the bike down on the ground.

For many, the downtube transfer is a faster technique because it requires less movement of the right arm. Start by grabbing the downtube with your right-hand and lift the bike from your shoulder (image 1). Allow your right elbow to slide out of the frame triangle and gently place the bike on the ground while slightly bending (image 2).

Either way, make sure you set the bike down gently. Do not drop it (image 3). Finally, remount the bike using the technique described in the standard carry section. Note that because the left crank arm was aligned with the chainstay during the run, the right pedal is in the perfect location for the remount. This pedal placement is particularly important when remounting on an incline, as you'll want to be able to apply power to the pedals as soon as possible to maintain forward momentum (image 4).

SHOULDERING DRILL

This drill has two variants. One is most suited for riders still mastering the skill of shouldering the bike. The other is great for those who have mastered the technique and want to perfect their shouldering and efficiency carrying the bike.

BASIC SHOULDERING LIFT DRILL (FINDING THE BEST TECHNIQUE FOR YOU):

Standing beside your bike, locate the midpoint of your downtube, about where your bottle cage bolts are located. After dismounting from the left side of the bike, place your right hand at the midpoint of the downtube and practice hoisting the bike up and onto your shoulder. You will notice that if your hand placement is too low it will cause your elbow to hit the seattube. If your hand placement is too high it will leave the bike unstable. Find the right balance point for the downtube lift by repeating this multiple times. Once you have found the balance point, now practice hoisting it and placing it on your shoulder. Once the bike is on your shoulder, practice removing it from your shoulder and placing it on the ground with the exact same hand placement. Note that you are not practicing the wrap just yet; you want to get the lift and lower perfected first then introduce the wrap. Practicing this multiple times will help imprint the muscle memory and get you used to feeling the pressure of the bike on your shoulder and the work required to lift it. For some riders, it helps to use your legs a bit more on the lift.

Now that you have tried the downtube lift, execute the same sequence of steps for the toptube lift. This will help you determine which method feels most natural for you and will help you learn a different method which might be more applicable for a barrier or run-up. First, find the optimal spot to lift your bike. Generally, this is almost in line with the nose of your saddle, which is typically the balance point of the bike and allows your elbow to clear the inside of the frame. Once you have found the proper lifting location, practice placing the bike on your shoulder using the toptube lift method. Then, practice removing the bike and placing it on the ground. Again, like the downtube lift, do this sequence multiple times.

Now mix the two techniques up. Lift the bike using the downtube lift and lower the bike using the toptube grip. Then lift the bike using the toptube lift and lower the bike using the downtube grip. Again, repeat this multiple times to really get used to the motion and to determine which style you prefer.

BASIC SHOULDERING WRAP DRILL (FINDING THE BEST TECHNIQUE FOR YOU):

Choose your preferred lift method and hoist the bike onto your shoulder. Now add in the wrap; first headtube wrap. Get used to the feeling of getting your arm around the headtube. For some, this method is initially difficult because of the reach required, but after practicing it a few times it turns out to be a comfortable method. For others it's not comfortable, and that is okay. Now practice your preferred lowering method. You'll notice that at first it will require a little bit of thought as to where you need to move your arm and place your hand. Practice the lift, wrap, and lower drill multiple times for your preferred lift method. Then practice the same sequence using the other lift method so you are experienced in both.

Now repeat the same drill using the downtube wrap. For some, this method is preferred because less reach is required and the placement of the bike on the shoulder is more comfortable. Again, repeat all iterations of the drill for both lift and lower methods.

Finally, choose which is your preferred lift method, preferred wrap method and preferred lower method, then repeat the sequence multiple times. By now you have probably lifted and placed the bike on your shoulder 30 times or more; this is perfect. The first time you do this drill your shoulder will be sore. It will also be sore for the next day or two, as there is a slight bruising that might occur. However repeating this drill for 5-10 minutes a week will quickly acclimate your body to the pressure of the bike, and you won't bruise or be sore once the race season arrives.

ADVANCED SHOULDERING DRILLS

Once you have mastered the basic lift and wrap drills, practice putting it all together in a fluid motion. Also, spend time running with the bike on your shoulder. It is recommended to master both lift techniques, as the toptube lift is generally preferred for fast dismounts, while the downtube lift is generally preferred for uphill dismounts.

FAST SHOULDERING DRILL:

Find a relatively smooth patch of grass or gravel and enter with moderate speed. Practice the standard dismount and toptube lift while focusing on maintaining your momentum. The fast shouldering drill may feel rushed at first. If so, start a bit slower so you feel in control and smooth, then incrementally increase your entering speed. Be sure to practice the entire sequence of dismount, toptube lift, wrap (whatever your preferred style might be), lower and remount. As a variant of this drill, run with the bike on your shoulder for an extended distance and add in a 180-degree turn, then run for a bit longer and remount. Be sure to practice both right-hand and left-hand turns to master where your body weight needs to be to make the turn in control. You can also include a turn, using your free hand to help you get around the tree or barrier faster.

UPHILL SHOULDERING DRILL:

Find a smooth patch of grass or gravel that leads into a fairly steep climb. Practice coming into the hill and carrying your momentum up the hill as you dismount the bike and execute a downtube lift. In the beginning you may want to start with a standard dismount, then move your hand down to the downtube. After you become comfortable moving your hand to the downtube, execute a dismount in which your right hand is placed directly onto your downtube—instead of the standard toptube placement—so you can transition directly from 3 points of contact with your hand on the downtube, to a lift. This is a good time to also practice pre-shifting before you dismount to make sure you are in the proper gear once you remount at the top of the hill or climb. Practice this drill multiple times to perfect your dismount, lift and remount. This drill also helps you become more comfortable running uphill with the bike on your shoulder, gradually becoming more efficient and making your whole process as smooth as possible.

SAND SHOULDERING DRILL:

Find a sandpit—beach volleyball courts generally work best—and practice your technique in a situation where your speed will be changing dynamically and your balance will be tested. Try entering the sandpit with some speed and executing your dismount in the sand. Notice how early or late you can dismount and still keep your momentum. Also try dismounting before entering the sandpit and note how your running stride changes as you transition from solid ground to soft sand. Your goal in this method should be to master the dismount and lift in the sand while maintaining maximum momentum. Sand in the drivetrain can have quite an effect on efficiency, especially if there is some moisture on the course or your bike. Use this drill to practice a "clean" dismount where your bike avoids all sand, and a "dirty" dismount where you ride your momentum into the sandpit before the dismount. At all times, however, you want to dismount before you stall. Coming to a stop at any obstacle on the course wastes precious seconds.

RUNNING DRILL:

For some in wet climates, shouldering and running are a regular part of racing. If you expect to be running quite a bit in races, find terrain similar to what you expect to be racing in—long hills, long sand sections, etc.—and practice running repeats with the bike on your shoulder. For a variant, remove the wheels from your bike then do the repeats. This allows you to focus on the running interval, especially early in the training phase. Once you have built up a good tolerance for the bike on your shoulder, you can put the wheels back on and do the intervals. While doing the drill, continue to focus on being smooth and practicing good technique in the dismount, lift, wrap, lower and remount. A common interval is to roll into the hill, shoulder and run up, then remount and roll back down to recover. Repeat eight times for one set. Start conservatively with a set, then start adding more as you get more comfortable and fit.

CORNERING

Corners in cyclocross are generally tighter than in your typical road race. The ground conditions may be slick or off-camber, where the ground is sloped away from the direction you are turning, like the opposite of a banked turn. Your ability to consistently ride corners at will go a long way toward determining your success in a race. Controlling your bike and maintaining speed through corners will save you time, and put pressure on racers trying to catch or keep up with you. Proficient cornering is a combination of picking the right line through a corner and executing it smoothly. You also save energy by not having to put in a big effort out of every corner to maintain your position in the race. One of the best ways to get faster at cornering is to follow a more experienced and faster rider through corners. You will notice that they tend to carry more speed into the turn because they know the limits of their tires better. Racers who ride corners well will also look through the turn to where they are going rather than looking at the corner. Meanwhile, they can also maximize their turning radius to carry as much speed as possible out of the corner.

If you do have to reduce your speed for a turn, it is better to do it immediately before the turn and not in the middle of the turn.

As with all features of the course, anticipate the gear you will need to be in after the turn and pre-shift before entering the turn. It is imperative that you are not over- or under-geared when you exit the turn so you can maintain your momentum and accelerate out of the turn smoothly without expending extra energy.

Try to maximize the radius of the turn by riding through the apex of the turn. Often you will hear the term 'tape-to-tape' (image 1). To do this, start from the outside of the turn (outside course-marking tape), go inside through the apex of the turn as close to the inside tape or stake as practical (image 2), and then exit on the outside of the turn (outside tape) (images 3 and 4). This keeps your line as straight as possible, maximizes your turning radius and allows you to carry more speed through the corner. By doing this, you also keep the bike more upright, resulting in more tread

contact. If you watch car or motorcycle racing, this line should be familiar to you.

Riding tape-to-tape is a best-case scenario. Conditions may dictate that a different line is faster. For instance, as the day progresses, the tape-to-tape line may become chewed up or filled with loose dirt that does not offer much traction. Taking an outside line along the tape may allow you to ride on grass the whole time and therefore gain better traction. As a result, you can get through the section faster by maintaining momentum even though you're going the long way.

Keep your head up and look at the exit of the turn. Your bike and body will follow your head.

Keep loose and relaxed through the turn. The bike may slide a bit under you. This is normal.

Keep corners in mind when dialing in tire pressure. Low pressure helps your tires grip the ground and keeps you from sliding. Tire pressure is too low when the tire folds under you at racing speeds, you usually want just a little more than that. Also, testing how fast you can get through tricky sections of the course is important during your pre-ride so that you know the speed limit of every corner.

Always think about the next course feature after the corner and adjust your line accordingly. If the next feature is a corner in the opposite direction, then fully going tape-to-tape is going to cause you to have a poor entrance angle for the next corner. In this case you want to adjust your line to maintain speed and maximize your turning radius while putting you in a good position to initiate the next turn, and again maximize your turning radius. The ability to anticipate the next feature is a key attribute in being able to carry the maximum speed through each feature and smoothly transition from one course section to the next.

HIGH-SPEED CORNERING (COUNTER-STEER)

A common road cycling technique is readily applied to high-speed turns in cyclocross: counter-steering. When entering a high-speed corner, your body lean dictates more of your turning motion than your tire steering into the turn. To properly negotiate a high-speed turn, a subtle maneuver is applied to initiate your body lean. As you approach the corner, apply slight pressure to the side of the handlebar that you are turning. For a fast right-hand corner, apply pressure to the right side of the handlebar, causing your wheel to turn slightly to the left. This has the effect of initiating your body and bike to lean to the right. The same principle applies for a left-hand turn. Once in the lean, it is a natural tendency for your body to balance the forces of each hand on the bars to keep you on track through the corner. As long as your eyes are looking toward where you want to go, your bike will follow. If you become fixated on an obstacle off your ideal path and stare at it, you will inevitably go right toward it. However if you trust your technique, you will ride the turn at a high rate of speed and carry momentum out of the corner.

Off-Camber

The off-camber turn is one in which the grade of the turn pulls you to the outside rather than to the inside. In most instances this means turning on a hill or downward slope. It's the opposite of a banked turn.

To successfully ride an off-camber section:

- Make sure you enter the off-camber turn at a speed you can maintain throughout. Too slow and you will lose traction, too fast and you will lose control of the bike. You should have figured out the right speed during your pre-ride.
- If you are following another rider into a tricky off-camber section, allow the rider some space. If the rider makes a mistake and slows down or abruptly stops you won't be delayed and you will have a better chance of passing safely.
- Do not brake through the turn. Doing so will disengage your tires from the ground and your chances of sliding are greater. It is also difficult to turn and brake at the same time.
- All factors being equal pick a high line on the off-camber to ride. This is not only the shortest route around the turn but it also gives you the most room with which to work. If you start high but can't stay there, you have room to move lower while keeping speed and traction. Starting too low doesn't give you that wiggle room and increases the chances that you will ride into the tape or have to pedal uphill. In short, it saves energy.
- Determine the best line during your warm up lap. Ride different lines on the off-camber and see what works best. Watch others ride and see where the popular line is and where the effective line is. Know the most effective line but also have an alternative line ready to go if race conditions dictate a change to your "A" plan.
- Sometimes the fastest way to ride an off-camber section is not to ride it at all. Remember the goal is who can get to the finish line first, not who can stay on their bike the longest. If the traction is questionable, practice dismounting and running your bike around the off-camber section. Keep in mind that if it is a steep off-camber where the high-side is on your right, running the bike can be a little tricky. You risk throwing off your balance and sliding down the hill. You have to either shoulder the bike or carry it a bit higher so that the wheels clear the ground. Dismounting and running tricky technical sections may be something you have to do on the first lap if you're not one of the first riders through the turn.

When entering the turn keep your body loose. Arms should be supple and ready to absorb the turn, your weight should be lightly on the saddle, predominantly on the downhill leg and slightly forward. The ability to keep weight on the front wheel, while pedaling for traction on the rear wheel, is generally the best method for off-camber corners.

By concentrating your weight to the outside, more of the tire tread will be forced to make contact with the ground. If your weight is on the inside, or hill side, less of the tread and more of the sidewall will contact the ground. This will increase the possibility that you are going to slide down the hill.

FINDING THE LINE

Keep in mind that the line that is burned in during the early races is not always the best line. If the Cat 4s or 5s and juniors go first, their speed will be lower and technique not as refined. They'll burn in a line that a lot of Cat 3s will follow because it's there, but a lot of time it's not a good line for their speed. By the time the elite race comes along, many of the racers completely ignore the burned in line. As with all techniques in 'cross, never just follow what everyone else does—evaluate for yourself and consider alternatives.

Tripod

Tripoding is an option that lays somewhere between running and riding. This method involves unclipping your uphill leg from the pedal and using it as an outrigger to keep the bike from slipping down the hill. This technique projects your center of gravity to the inside of the turn so you don't have to lean your body as much, and therefore your bike as much, resulting in a
better tread contact patch.

The unclipped leg should be out in front of you and not straight down. If it is out in front and you have to catch yourself by touching down, there is less of a chance you will bounce.

This technique should be used conservatively and is best for super-slippery turns that may be quicker to run. Tripoding can get you around a turn quickly and could be a viable option but it comes with a couple caveats.

- It is harder to keep your body loose, absorbing the shock of the terrain, while you have a foot unclipped from the pedal.
- Conditions in which you are going to unclip and tripod may be muddy and possibly frozen. Clipping back in to the pedal in these conditions is never easy. You may end up saving time by tripoding and losing it all back when you can't clip back into the pedal.
- Sometimes running is faster and less risky. Don't be afraid to run.
- "Fred Flintstone" hybrid technique, in which you stay on your bike but kick the ground to move forward, is an option for long, off-camber traverses.

Like mud and sand, off-camber turns are another course feature in which you have to have confidence and even a little faith that your tires are going to do their job. If you feel your tires start to slip, don't immediately try to brake, turn or otherwise make a save. Instead, stay calm, don't tense up, and let the tires do their job. In most instances after a slight drift many tires will re-grip and get you back on track. If your tires consistently slip on off-camber turns without hooking back up, you may want to look into using tires with more aggressive side knobs on the tread.

CORNERING DRILL

Practicing on different corners over and over with different tire pressures is something that a lot of people don't do. Set up different types of corners to practice on and purposely try to determine what tire pressures work for you on that type of corner. Start off at 32 psi, drop by 5 psi and ride the corner again. Drop by another 5 psi and do it again. Maybe add 2 psi to your tires to go up again. Do it until you find the ideal tire pressure for that type of corner. That way on race day, you have a frame of reference to go off of when choosing your tire pressure.

PEANUT DRILL

The peanut drill works solo or for a group. On an open patch of grass, either flat or on a slight hillside, place 8 cones—or water bottles—in a large peanut shape. Begin the drill by focusing on anticipating the next feature, in this case entry into a corner in the other direction. Work on maximizing your turning radius and maintaining speed throughout the corners. The first goal is to complete the peanut (in as wide of a configuration as you wish) without touching the brakes in one direction. Remember to look through each turn, in this case, it is best to look at least one cone ahead. Complete multiple laps, then repeat the drill in the opposite direction. The outside corners are opportunities for higher speed turns, whereas the interior corners generally require a slower, tighter turn. The next goal is to focus on applying some pressure to the pedals (accelerating) as you exit the turns, while still maintaining the goal of not braking through the course. Eventually you will start going so fast that you will have to start scrubbing speed before you initiate the next turn.

If you find yourself braking through the apex of the turn, slow it down and progress again. You always want to brake before the turn, not during the turn. If possible, add another rider and start on opposite sides of the peanut and race each other. At first, end the race when one rider catches up to the wheel of the other; when you are comfortable you can later end the race when one rider passes the other. In this scenario you'll have to work on setting up the pass and executing it safely, similar to the strategic cornering drill earlier. You can also do this drill with a small group of riders, which will teach you how to ride through a group, pass, and maintain your technique while others are taking the optimal line away. A final modification to this drill is to shrink the peanut such that the cornering is much tighter, requiring much more body English to navigate the tight turns. While this may not seem at first to have as many direct race applications, understanding how you can manipulate your bike with your body weight is a key attribute in handling off-camber turns, mud, sand, snow, ice and loose gravel.

FIGURE EIGHT DRILL

Find a hillside and place a cone (or bottle) ten feet down the hill. Practice riding down the hill, around the cone and back up the hill. Change the angle of your entry and exit. Add extra cones to restrict the angle of entry and exit. Also, turn around and go the other direction so that you are leaning to the other side. You may find it's easier for you to turn one direction more than the other. Spend more practice time riding your weaker direction. Another drill is to set up two cones on the hillside about thirty feet away from each other. Then ride a figure eight pattern around the two cones. Switch directions on this drill about halfway through your drill time.

EASTON
EASTON
EASTON
EASTON

SAND

A sand section in a cyclocross race is usually a focal point of the course. It's a fun challenge to ride and also a place where spectators like to watch displays of technical skill and the possibility of crashes. Similar to the mud, all sand is not created equally. It can be deep, heavy and almost impossible to ride through, or it can be shallow, loose and a breeze to fly right through. Like every other obstacle in 'cross, a sand section is an obstacle that requires decision-making. Ultimately you want to find the fastest, most efficient way to get through the sand.

Similar to almost every topic discussed in this book, many of the decisions you make on how to approach a sand section need to be addressed during your pre-race laps. Before riding into a sand section, pull over and watch other riders. See if it is easy to ride or if everybody is running. There may be a good line that has formed in the sand that you want to take advantage of, or an area that isn't as deep or heavy that should be avoided. This is the type of information that is easy to collect by observation rather than riding. But also keep in mind that lines in the sand are fleeting. They will change throughout the day and may disappear completely if the race organizer grooms the sand between races.

That being said, sand is not a place to be a trailblazer. If there is an established line, use it. It takes a lot less energy to ride the sand where somebody else has already cleared the way than it does to start a fresh path.

Riding sand is all about momentum and forward motion. If you get bogged down, you will have to dismount. An unplanned dismount in the middle of a sand section is slower than running the whole section would've been because you have come to a complete stop and lost all momentum. However, a strategically planned dismount can be a fast and effective way of traversing a longer sandpit. If you are not confident that you can ride the entire sand section, it is fine to get off and run part of the way through, as long as your dismount is planned and you do it while still rolling forward so you can keep momentum.

Also consider running the section instead of riding if there is a hill or other demanding course feature after the sand section. If riding sand takes so much out of you that you need to use the section immediately after to recover—and the terrain does not allow for it—consider running instead. That way you can steady your effort and have enough energy left to attack the climb or other difficult feature.

Wet sand can wreak havoc on a bike's drivetrain and brakes. For that reason some riders choose to run a sand section—assuming it's not slower—to avoid fouling their bike. Many riders don't have a pit bike, or if they do, they don't have a professional mechanic handing it up to them every lap after cleaning the sand off. Preserving your bike can often become a factor in choosing how to ride certain sections.

Before entering the sand make sure you are in a gear that has you spinning at a higher than normal cadence. Once in the sand, the effort will become harder, so you want to make sure you are still able to turn the pedals over. If you try to change gears while in the sand, more times than not it won't end well and you will quickly find yourself dismounting and running.

When you enter the sand, your speed is going to drop dramatically. Make sure that your weight is back a bit more than you originally anticipate so that when you enter the sand you don't get pitched over the bars. Although only "naturally occurring" sand is supposed to be used in UCI events, for non-UCI events, man-made sandpits are legal. Many of these have a distinct elevation drop from the grass to the sand. In these instances, keeping your weight far back is crucial when entering the sand section. Also make sure that you are not going too fast on entry because you do not want to brake once you enter the sand. Braking, especially the front wheel, will disrupt your balance by shifting your weight forward, moving you from your desired line and possibly causing you to have to dismount.

Pedaling in the sand is an important key to success. There is no coasting in the sandpit! Keep a moderately high cadence, keep the pedal stroke smooth with constant power, and don't stop turning the pedals over until you exit the sand. Even a half pedal-stroke pause can lose enough momentum to make the difference between clearing the sand, or having to dismount and run.

Keep your upper body loose. Tensing your arms and shoulders can throw you off balance and it makes it harder to react to subtle changes in the terrain. Also, keep your weight back, either on the saddle or hovering above it, such that you have about two-thirds of your weight distributed to the back of the bike. This allows the front wheel to float over the sand instead of digging into any depressions, ruts, or soft spots that could throw you off balance. If you move forward or stand, you will unweight the rear wheel and lose traction. Your head should remain up and your eyes should focus on the exit point from the sand. There is no need to look at the sand. If you drop your head, your weight will shift forward and the front wheel will dig into the sand, slowing your momentum and possibly bringing you to a stop.

Keep your hands on the hoods or tops of the handlebars and keep them loose. You will not have complete control over where your bike wants to go in the sand. You are more guiding the bike than steering it and sometimes the bike is going to go where it wants. Again, let the front end float, and use your body weight, rather than moving the handlebars, to keep the bike under control. Be prepared for this and fight the urge to overcorrect. Balance and momentum will keep you on course. Continue to keep your eyes on your exit point and the bike will follow along. To as much of an extent as possible, let the bike find its own line.

Some courses will include a turn in the middle of the sandpit. If the course is damp and the sand is packed down, riding the turn may be an option. However, turning in the sand will most likely result in dramatic slowing. The front wheel may forge straight ahead, bog down or wash out completely. In this instance, planning a mid-sand dismount and run may be the fastest option.

Sand Running

If you decide running is the quickest, most efficient path through the sand, you must make that decision well in advance of the obstacle. Deciding last second to dismount is going to be inefficient and slow. Once you have committed to running, dismount in the same manner as described in the dismount section. For short sand sections, the standard carry is acceptable. For longer sections, where you will be running a good distance, shouldering the bike is the best choice because it puts you into an efficient running position. It's almost never OK to push the bike through the sand, the extra energy required is simply not worth it. When running through sand, use small quick steps. Also, pump your free arm to help keep you moving forward.

There is no penalty for running in somebody else's footprints. In fact, this may be the quickest way to travel because the sand is compacted and easier to run on. While running keep your head up and lean slightly forward. Once out of the sand, gently place your bike back on the ground, remount and go.

Often the fastest way through a long sand section is to enter it riding, planning on a mid-sandpit dismount and run. The key is to dismount while you still have momentum, well before you come to a near stop. As a general rule, if you begin to lose excessive speed and get bogged down, dismount and run instead of burning needless energy trying to ride the sand. Running will save your legs for the rest of the race, instead of churning out 50rpm and fighting with balance. This is also an instance when being able to dismount, pick up the bike and carry it all in a short period of time becomes a crucial skill, and it's why we spent so much time earlier in the book explaining the nuances of those techniques.

SAND AND BIKE MAINTENANCE

It may go without saying, but sand is not good for your bike. It gets into your drivetrain and can quickly affect performance. If you do ride the sand in practice, make sure you have enough time to thoroughly clean your bike (specifically the chain, chainrings, rear cassette and rear derailleur jockey wheels) before the race begins.

SAND ENTRANCE DRILL:

Find a sand section similar to what you may experience in a race, such as a beach volleyball court at your local park. Approach the sandpit with moderate speed and keep your weight back as you transition from grass to sand. Try to maintain as much momentum as possible such that you make it across the short length of the sandpit. Remember that not only do you need to keep your weight back on the entry, but you also need to practice keeping your weight toward the back of the bike to allow the front wheel to float over the undulations in the sand to keep your balance and forward momentum.

SAND TURNS DRILL:

Generally, turning in sand is a difficult task unless the sand is slightly moist or there have been enough riders going through it to pack it down. Repeat the sand entrance drill, but this time add in a turn halfway through the sandpit. At first the turn will be fairly shallow. Stay close to the parallel edge of the sandpit so you can turn toward the grass and exit the sandpit after a short period. Gradually move farther from the sandpit edge and try to work up to a 90-degree turn. Be sure to practice turning both left and right, and remember that you are going to be controlling the bike more from body weight than from hard turns on the handlebars.

SAND RUNNING DRILL:

Similar to the sand entrance drill, enter the sandpit with moderate speed, however this time execute a dismount as you begin to lose your momentum. Practice both the standard dismount and carry (preferred for short running section) and the dismount to shoulder (for longer sand sections). Generally you will want to lower the bike and remount after you have cleared the sand. Practice good technique on these skills to further imprint the smooth, fast techniques you have learned.

IMPORTANT NOTE ON SAND:

Sand is harsh on your drivetrain. Try to do these drills when your bike is dry and clean, and make sure to thoroughly clean your bike after the drill. In some cases, only a few passes through a sandpit will require the removal and cleaning of your bottom bracket and crankset. Don't skimp on the cleaning if you have been doing sand work, a little time invested can save you money.

MUD

If you tell an experienced 'cross racer that a course is muddy, expect to be asked "what kind of mud is it?" As you begin racing in adverse conditions you quickly realize that all mud is not created equally. It can range from a thin silt that gets you dirty but doesn't really slow you down to heavy thick mud that accumulates on your bike and makes racing conditions extremely hard. Peanut butter, Play-Doh, slime, goop, glop, soup: all of these terms are used, albeit inconsistently, to describe muddy conditions on a 'cross course.

Preparation is key to racing in mud. Having a functional bike is more important than finding the best line. If you are racing in extremely muddy conditions, having a spare bike and a friend working for you in the pit is a game changer. Thick mud—especially when combined with loose grass—and frozen mud, will get stuck in your drivetrain; clog up your brakes; make clipping in and out of pedals difficult; accumulate on tires; and add pounds to your bike. By the end of a race your 18-pound bike could easily weigh 40 pounds and the wheels will most likely not spin. If you are really unlucky, your race may end prematurely with a broken rear derailleur hanger. This is not an uncommon issue in severely muddy conditions.

If you have a pit person, make sure you provide that person with a bucket with warm water and brushes to use. Some courses have power washers in the pits, but most local races do not. Be prepared.

If you do not have a pit person, it is still a good idea to bring a spare bike, wheels or at the very least, a bucket with water and brushes. If you can no longer pedal your bike, taking a minute to clean it in the pits during the race may be faster than trying to deal with a mud clogged machine on course.

POWER WASHER

A great addition to your home service course is a portable power washer. There are models that plug into the 12-volt socket in your car. The tank holds enough to quickly clean off two bikes and with a battery pack, the unit is portable and you could put it by the pits. A low tech alternative is a five gallon bucket, a brush, and a water bottle to provide a jet stream of water.

Before the race it is best to test the conditions and see what is going to work best for you in the mud. However, you may make the decision that warm-up laps are more detrimental than useful. If you do not have a spare bike, and there are no bike-washing facilities, or really long lines for the pressure washers or hoses, not riding the course before your race may be the best bet. In instances such as these, at least walk the course, along the side, outside the course tape, so you are still as prepared as possible.

Arriving at the start line with a clean bike rather than one already clogged with mud is more important than pre-riding the course. In this type of situation, in which you do not have an opportunity to clean your bike pre-race, walk the course and watch other racers take different lines, especially the muddy parts, talk to other racers about how they handled the conditions, and warm up on the road or the trainer.

The most important key to riding mud may be mental: believe that you can ride it. Even go as far as telling yourself it is a strength and something you can use to your advantage. This belief and confidence many times will have you riding stronger and faster through the mud. If you are tentative, you will slow down and lose momentum making the section much harder.

To ride through mud, keep your hands on the tops of the handlebars or the hoods. Your body should be upright and your weight back. Slide to the back of the saddle or even hover slightly above it. The goal is to keep most of your weight near the rear of the bike so you do not lose traction and start to spin the rear wheel. Try to keep steady power to the rear wheel, avoiding any power surges, which might break your traction of the mud.

Keep a light grip on the bars and let the steering float a little bit. Staying loose in your upper-body improves balance and breathing. This makes you faster and more efficient. As you ride through the mud, your bike will not travel in a straight line. To counteract this, keep your body square to the exit and always move forward. This will keep your body stable, even if your bike is not.

Let the front wheel float and look where you want to go. Allow the bike to move under you and use your body weight to shift your balance to control the bike. Also, do not assume that the path that everyone is riding is the fastest one, it often ends up that the main path gets rutted out more, while the path on the edges isn't as deep and has more solid grip. If your tire slots into a rut, follow the rut with your eyes, as you are not getting out of it and you will go where you look. This is called "committing to the rut."

If the mud is on a flat and straight section of the course, be in a gear you can spin and enter the section at a comfortable speed. Do not unnecessarily slow down before the mud section. Momentum is your friend. Also, do not brake or change gears. Neither of these actions should be necessary in a flat muddy section as long as you have chosen a gear that you can turn over. If it is too easy, continue at a high cadence through the mud and make the adjustment on the next lap.

This may sound counterintuitive but using a bigger gear that takes a little more effort to spin is better for thick mud. Pushing a bigger gear requires more downward force on the pedals, which pushes the rear wheel deeper into the mud. In many instances this will improve traction. It also lessens the possibility of spinning the rear wheel.

When turning in slick mud, make your turning radius as long as possible, and even try to pre-turn on a patch of solid ground before the turn so you can straighten the turn out even more.

If the mud is so thick and deep that riding is difficult, do not hesitate to get off your bike and run. Running muddy sections in many instances is faster than riding. If you have ever watched a muddy World Cup race, you will see the pros run a lot. There are sections that seem like they are perfectly rideable that the pros do not even think about riding. They know it is quicker to run and that their bikes will be cleaner and, therefore, faster once they remount.

Riding on a muddy off-camber section is tricky. In many instances, running is faster. Even if it is a fraction slower, if your bike remains less muddy than those who choose to ride the mud, you may be faster than the competition once you remount. If you do decide to run, using toe spikes in your shoes is important. These screw in spikes come in many shapes and sizes, depending on the conditions, and greatly improve traction when running and climbing in slippery conditions.

For a muddy off-camber section, you want to place most of your weight on the outside or downhill pedal and your bike and body should be almost parallel to the hillside. This will place your tire at an angle that provides the largest contact patch. You will need to lean your upper-body a bit into the hill to keep your balance. Remember: pedal, pedal pedal. Keeping momentum here is the most important thing. If the bike changes lines on its own, don't overcorrect. Sometimes your machine dictates where you are going to go. Learn to accept this.

Sometimes muddy off-camber sections are too steep to pedal a full revolution. In other words, the pedal on the uphill side strikes the ground on the downstroke. If this happens and you do not want to dismount and run, you have two options. You can unclip your hillside shoe and kick-push the bike. The outside shoe should remain clipped in and at the 6 o'clock position. You can also pedal half-revolutions. Start your hillside pedal at 9 o'clock and pedal to 3 o'clock. Then pedal backwards from 3 to 9 and repeat.

Tire pressure and tread selection are extremely important for muddy courses. This is where you need to do some experimentation to figure out what works best. Different tread patterns will handle mud differently, if you have options, experiment with them. The tire you think should work best may not perform as well as other options. Lower tire pressure is always going to be better. It will give the bike better traction and also allow for more mud to be shed from the bike as you ride. If you are riding tubular tires, tire pressure as low as 12 to 15 psi can be run on extremely muddy courses.

On a muddy course vegetation is your friend. Grass and vegetation have roots that go deep into the mud and muck. If it's not the type of mud that collects heavily on your bike, looking to ride on areas with some vegetation generally will provide the most traction. Also look for solid obstacles to use for traction, such as the base of a small tree, the gravelly rocks on the edge of the trail or anything solid that you can get your tires to hook up on.

If there are puddles on the course that you can ride through, use them to your advantage. A quick way to shed clogged mud from a bike is to ride through a big puddle. Just make sure you do this in practice first. You never want to be surprised about how deep or what lies at the bottom of a puddle during a race.

Also, if there is a long running section on the course where you are shouldering the bike, you can use it as an opportunity to clear mud from your bike. Most importantly, clear the mud from underneath your fork and seat stays and around the brakes to give the tire more clearance to spin.

MUD DRILLS

Practicing mud-riding is a tricky balance. You want to practice the skill, but you don't want to destroy your local trails or parks. Use discretion and your best judgment when deciding to do mud drills.

As the saying goes, the first step in becoming a good mudder is believing that you are a good mudder. Self-confidence makes a huge difference, and experience in the mud certainly helps.

If you have an accessible section of mud, first practice holding a straight line through the section by properly weighting the bike, keeping your focus on where you want to go and keeping your weight rearward. Let your front wheel float. It may find its way into a rut or it may float over them—either way keep your momentum moving forward.

Next, either find a muddy turn, or make a turn in your mud section, and practice entering the section straight, then initiating a turn in the mud. This is a much different sensation than on grass or gravel. The turn requires much more feel and body weight shifts. As always, be sure to look where you want to go and keep your power output smooth. Repeat the turn in both directions multiple times, each time trying to carry even more speed. At some point you will start to lose traction. Practice pushing the limit of your cornering ability in the mud and get accustomed to the sensation of your tires slipping. This will also help you learn to save the slips so you don't crash into the mud. Once you reach your perceived limit of speed through the turn, try it again using the tripod method and see if you can enter with more speed and carry the momentum through the muddy turn. This drill also poses a great opportunity to experiment with different tire pressure, so if possible, bring your pump and tire gauge with you to the drills practice session.

With so many different types of mud, the best way to get faster in all of them is to get more comfortable with handling your bike in any slippery terrain. The more time you spend drilling and practicing in mud, the more comfortable you will be in how your bike handles, and therefore you can carry more speed with more confidence.

CYCLOCROSS SEASON PREPARATION

When you approach preparation for the 'cross season, your training should really start right after your previous season ended. The first thing that needs to be done is to take a look at what kind of training you did over the course of the previous year. What did you do in the spring, summer, and early fall to get ready for 'cross season? What did you do during race season? Hopefully you kept a journal so you can look back and see specifically what you were doing and how you reacted to it. If you have never raced 'cross before, great! You are a blank canvas and can hopefully pick up some tips on how to prepare for your upcoming 'cross season.

When you look at the "off season" (typically February through August) you have seven months to get ready for the next 'cross season. If you have been racing every weekend since the season started, the first thing you should do is relax, kick back, hang out with friends and family and don't do anything training related for a week or two. This break should help "reset" you to training again. If you didn't race, then you need to start off with a couple of months of base training. We aren't going to spell everything out in this book or give you specific daily workouts but the overview should help get you started. The following descriptions are based on a person's season starting in mid-September.

February—The season is over and it's time to relax, but don't get too comfortable. Although rest and recovery are crucial and having a week or two weeks away from the bike or training in general is important, February should be spent working on all those thing you have been ignoring since the 'cross season started. If you have a core, yoga or strength routine that you did last year, now is the time to start it up again. If you didn't, now is the perfect time to talk to some friends to see what they do or go to your local gym and see what they offer. However, remember to take it slowly and ease yourself into your program. You are most likely going from little to no yoga, strength or core to a full-on routine. You don't want to injure yourself by being too aggressive. February is the perfect time for core work since it can be done inside at a time when the majority of the northern hemisphere is cold and damp. Riding is important this month but it could be a case where you are just riding 3 or 4 times per week.

March—Hopefully the weather has turned and you can spend some quality time outside. You should be continuing to do your core, yoga and strength routines on a multiple-times-per-week basis as well as increasing the amount of time you are spending on your bike. Doing group rides or long solo rides—as well as starting to do intervals again—are key for this month. More likely than not, your local road or mountain bike race season starts this month. It can't hurt to get out there and do some of these races for fun. Remember that many roadies were doing their base training back in November and December while you were racing. So don't be too critical of yourself if you are not in top form.

April and May—These two months are where you are going to get the type of training that is going to allow you to train at higher intensities in the late summer. Two to three longer rides at a higher pace per week in addition to two threshold type intervals are key for this month. Keep continuing to do your core, yoga and strength routines 2-3 days per week.

June and July—The months of June and July are critical to your prep work for the season. In addition to 2-3 long rides per week, you want to start adding in some high-intensity short-duration intervals (in July) to start working on those energy systems that you rely on heavily during the 'cross season. You also want to be working on that middle of the road threshold zone, as this is one of the main crucial components in determining your performance. As far as 'cross technique is concerned, you want to spend June reintroducing yourself to your 'cross bike and the basic skills that we covered in this book. July is the time that you want to correct any mistakes that you are making in your dismount, remount, or cornering. Also make sure to take a break from riding. A planned recovery week every 4-6 weeks is just as important as interval work and the longer, higher-intensity rides throughout the year. You can't keep building yourself up with out taking the time to let your body adapt.

August—You want to be spending this month tweaking your form for the season as well as getting in a few final long distance rides. Once the season starts, you may have to give those up during the week to recover from racing on the weekend. In addition to the long distance rides, you also want to be continue to do those high-intensity short-duration intervals. Finally, you want to be working on 'cross-specific technique 2-3 days per week to refine what you have been working on since June.

September through December—Racing starts again. Once racing starts, you have to find a good balance between rest, recovery and training so that you stay fit for the season and are able to race to the best of your ability on the weekend. The thing to keep in mind for the race part of the year is that if you are racing on Sunday, you may not be recovered until Tuesday so the first hard day of training won't be until Wednesday. If you are racing on Saturday and Sunday, push that schedule forward by a day and you may not be training until Thursday. As you can see, it can quickly get complicated. Just remember, at this point in the season you hopefully have put in months of solid training previously and that for right now, less is more. If there happens to be a weekend in which there isn't any racing, that may be the perfect opportunity to get in some longer 3-4 hour rides since you most likely haven't done any since the summer time. Having an extra day of recovery couldn't hurt either.

PART 2
RACING

BEFORE THE RACE

Being in the best shape of your life and ready to slay the competition will only pay off if you show up to the race with your shoes, helmet, bike and everything else you need. Granted, the cyclocross community is close knit enough that in most cases teammates and friends will help you cobble together any essential gear you may have forgotten. But scrambling around for a pair of socks or bibshorts moments before your race starts will leave you distracted and in a negative mental state.

Successful racers are meticulous in their preparation. Regular racers all know of that one guy who is a complete mess moments before the race starts, yet always seems to perform well, but he is the exception and not the rule. Just think how much better that disorganized racer may do in a race if he had time to concentrate on a proper warm-up and course recon rather than where he left his sunglasses.

If you are packing your gear bag moments before leaving for the race venue, you're doing it wrong. All of your clothing, tools, food, helmet, shoes, glasses, spare parts and bike should be ready to go 48 hours before a race. Some riders' gear bags never get fully unpacked, they just rotate in appropriate clothing for each particular race.

Make a checklist of all the gear you need for the race in your gear bag. There is an extensive list of gear with descriptions and uses starting on page 87. You can also keep a second copy of the checklist taped to the inside of your door. That way, before you leave for the race, you can peruse the list to make absolutely sure nothing is left behind. There's something else implicit in all this—have a gear bag. A simple duffel can do it or you can buy a sport-specific bag with pockets and compartments designed to keep all the gear you need. A little daypack or a canvas shopping bag isn't going to hold all of the gear we recommend.

Prepare Early

The first thing to remember about race day is that it really should begin two nights prior. A best practice is to make sure everything is packed and ready to go 48 hours before the event. That way you are not up late the night before a race. On the night before the race, everything is packed in the car or by the door ready to go. Keep your gear bag and everything else you need to take to the race in one place. Line up your bags, tools, floor pump, trainer and bikes all in front of the door. Leave them in a way that makes it impossible for you to leave without stepping over everything. That way there is less of a chance that anything will be left behind. One more item that should be on your list—and is something you should take care of well in advance—is directions to where the race will be held. Do not wait until you get into the car to figure out where you need to go. Look at a map the night before. Put the address in a GPS device and print out instructions as a back-up.

Once everything is in the car or by the door, go to sleep. Early. Shoot for at least eight hours of sleep. For most of us that is an impossible feat but it's worth setting as a goal. There is no easier performance enhancer than sleep. Going in to your race day fresh and rested is invaluable. Before you go to sleep, make sure you set your alarm. Give yourself plenty of extra time in the morning. You do not want to be rushed. It's worth noting that research shows sleep (duration and quality) 2 nights before an important event is more critical than sleep the night before.

Food Is Fuel

After you wake up and go through your morning routine, it's time to eat. Getting a good breakfast of the "right" foods on race day ranks right up there with sleep: Easy to accomplish and really important. There are many options for breakfast. You want to make sure you ingest enough calories and enough carbohydrates to get you through the first part of the day. If you are racing in the morning it's also important to avoid eating a big meal less than three hours before the race. A meal of steel cut oats (a slow burning carbohydrate) with nuts and fruit is a typical breakfast many bike racers live by. Throw in some peanut butter or eggs and it's a meal that can keep you full for hours.

JPOW TIP Keep the timing and content of your pre-race meal consistent. It should be something that you can make anywhere—at home, on the road, in a hotel or at host housing.

Breakfast is also a good time to think about your race plan; not necessarily how you will attack specific features on the course but how you want to approach the race as a whole. The more you race, the more detailed the race plan becomes. In general, you want to think about how you are going to dose your efforts, if you are going to try and jump up to the lead pack then hang on, or if you are going to conserve in the first few laps to let the pack shake out and make your move later. The reason behind formulating a plan is to always race with a purpose. Having a purpose leads to more decisive behavior, which is nearly always faster. Also, if you've already considered possibilities before the race and decided how to handle them, it cuts down on the thinking you have to try to do while you're going full gas in a race. Finally, thinking about the details of racing shifts your brain away from the 'how will I do?' anxiety-provoking thoughts, and on to more productive thoughts about executing your best race.

Now it's time to pack the car and get on the road. Remember that list you made? Make sure you check it one more time before leaving the house. There's nothing worse than getting halfway to the race before remembering you left your helmet on the kitchen counter.

Arrive At The Venue

When you arrive at the venue try to find a parking spot that offers you as many of the following as possible: close to course access; close to registration; close to the starting grid; on level ground (this is nice if you plan on warming up on a trainer); access to bathroom facilities; access to bike wash or hose, especially on messy days.

You have invested hours and hours of time in your fitness, a good amount of money in your equipment, and in some instances you have even driven hours to and from each race. So why show up just in time to hop out of the car, get pinned up, spin around the parking lot a few times and head to the line? If you have invested this much time, effort and money into the sport, do yourself a huge favor and invest an additional 90 minutes of your day getting to the race site early. In a perfect world, you will arrive to the venue two to three hours before your race. This amount of time allows you to change clothes, warm up, register, pin your number to your jersey, get some pre-race food and concentrate on your race. It allows you to do all of these things without rushing. Also remember that aside from competition, race day is often a social event. You are going to see folks in the parking lot that you haven't seen in a week or longer and it's

BUDDY SYSTEM

If you are new to racing, one of your pre-season assignments is to find a veteran and ask if you can become that person's race-day shadow. Whatever they do, you do, too. Eventually, you may come up with your own system but if you have no idea what's going on, watching somebody who has been racing a while is a great way to learn. So where do you meet this person you are going to shadow? The best bet is at your local cyclocross practice. A nice by-product of the sport's growing popularity is that many places now have weekly, informal, cyclocross practices. Ask around at your local bike shop or on your local bike racing list-serve to find out where practices are held. These sessions are invaluable. They will help hone the skills needed to compete and plug you into the cyclocross scene.

If you can't find a practice or somebody to tag along with at a race, it's not the end of the world. One of the best ways to figure out the sport is to watch it. Instead of showing up, racing, packing up the car and going home, stick around for a while. Watch the other fields and figure out the dos and don'ts of the sport. Guaranteed you will see plenty of both. If possible, stay at the venue long enough to watch the elite races. This is where you are going to see the sport performed technically correctly and at high speeds.

Unlike a stadium sport, nobody is going to stop you from changing seats when you are watching a 'cross race. Take advantage of this. Watch the riders at the start. Move to the barriers. Check out how they ride off-cambers and what technique they use to shoulder the bike on run-ups. So much can be learned by watching the top riders, yet most people don't stick around to watch them race. This is an easy way to get some secret knowledge over your competitors.

tough to not stop and chat. Make sure you work in a little extra time for a bit of pre-race socializing. Also make sure you factor in to your schedule the possibility that you may have to wait in line to pick up your number.

Organizing a race is not an easy task and in most areas the folks working registration, as well as everywhere else at the venue, are volunteers. The sport is also growing by leaps and bounds. These factors can result in a bit of a back up to register at some races. The number one thing to remember in these situations is to not get angry. Delays happen and you need to roll with it. If you've given yourself that extra time, you can combine pre-race socializing and line-waiting into the same activity.

Once you have parked the car, your next step is going to rely on the time. One item you should keep in your gear bag is a daily event schedule. If you are racing in a series, the daily schedule most likely will not change from week to week.

If you are racing in the first race of the day, this isn't as important. You should arrive with plenty of time before your race starts to complete several laps of the course, register, pin on your number, get a warm up in, make sure the bike is in working order, dial in the tire pressure and roll to the line.

If, however, you are racing in a later race, you should check the schedule to see what is happening on the course when you have arrived. If a race is just about to end, you should quickly change into clothes you are comfortable wearing to ride the course. This can be jeans and a t-shirt if that works for you. As long as you have your helmet and shoes on, everything else really doesn't matter if the course is about to be open for preview. If you have time to change into a kit, do that. Remember, this is why you want to bring at least two kits and two pairs of shoes, if you own them. Even at slow pace you will sweat during your warm up lap. And if the course is muddy you will appreciate having a clean kit and a dry pair of shoes to wear. If it is wet and muddy it is important that you stay both warm and dry before your race.

Warming Up And Course Reconnaissance

At most races you are allowed to enter the race course to warm up as soon as the winner crosses the finish line. There are three important points to keep in mind when starting a warm-up lap. First, make sure you enter the course after the finish line and not before the winner has crossed the line. In many series the race announcer will inform you when the course is open. Second, there will still be racers finishing their final lap on the course when you start your warm-up. It is important that you do not pass these riders or enter the course in front of them. It's good sportsmanship to let everybody have the opportunity to finish the race unencumbered. Third, never cross the finish line on a warm-up lap. The officials are trying to score hundreds, if not thousands of racers throughout the day. If you cross the finish line during your warm-up lap, they are going to be trying to make out your number, find you on the lap tally, and give you a placing. All of this distracts officials from their hectic job of compiling results from the previous race. Well-organized events have specific gaps in the schedule dedicated as pre-ride times. Find the one that works best for you and use it.

This first warm-up lap is not a time to go race pace, also known as a "hot lap," instead you want to ride at a moderate pace and concentrate on the course. Remember how we talked about how racing has a social component to it and you need to work some time into your schedule to socialize and chat? Your first warm-up lap is not that time. Too many riders will mindlessly ride around the course having a chat with their buddies instead of paying attention to the terrain. If the course is set up correctly, you will have to make decisions on how to ride certain sections. Before the race, rather than during it, is when you want to be figuring this out.

Something you will hear racers talking about is lines. As in "the right side of the course is the better line through the mud," or "take the lower line around that turn." A line is the path you follow as you go around the course. When you are riding the course for the first time, the goal is to find the best lines, the ones that will get you around the course the fastest. Many times a natural line will start to form. You will see the path carved out in the ground from all the previous riders. However, you need to be familiar with alternative lines, as well. If everybody has figured out the same best line, you may get an advantage by taking a different route and not getting caught in traffic. Also, as conditions change, the best line may change. This means that you want to be really familiar with the tricky parts of the course. If there is a particular section, say a steep off-camber turn that seems difficult to ride, during your warm-up lap is the time to dial in that section. Nothing is stopping you from riding a certain part of the course multiple times while warming up. For instance, for that tricky off-camber, you can ride it once up high, then duck under the course tape, reverse course to before the turn, get back on the course and ride it again, this time going low. Then you can duck under the tape again and not ride, but watch other racers attempt the same section. Watch closely what other riders do. Are they using different lines? Which one seems to be fastest? Is it the same line you chose? If you're lucky, you may see some of the men and women who will be racing the elite race getting in some early warm-up laps. These are the folks to keep a close eye on. If none of those riders are at the venue that early, it is still worthwhile to stick around and watch them race, too. It's a great way to confirm that your instincts were correct or to learn what to look for next time if the best riders are all approaching a section differently than you did.

Early races are usually lower category racers, and they usually just follow each other around the course, not really thinking about what lines are optimal. A great example of this is a muddy corner that eventually becomes barely rideable on the inside, where all the racers have chewed it up. However, the outside is often still nice and grippy, allowing you to carry more momentum even after the lower categories are done racing. The lesson is, don't just pay attention to the already-ridden line, look to both sides while you're riding as well. The shortest line is not always the fastest line in cyclocross racing, sometimes it's a longer line that allows you to hold more momentum and avoid costly re-accelerations or even to stay on your bike rather than dismounting and running. Likewise, there are situations where dismounting and running an entire section can be both faster and safer than trying to ride it. Even at the top levels, you will sometimes see professionals get off and run sections that they could ride 50% of the time. They don't need to risk crashing every single lap.

TUBULAR VS. CLINCHERS

In cyclocross, you want to run your tires with lower pressure than on the road. Lower pressure increases traction and efficiency. However, if you are running clincher tires, a beaded tire with an inner-tube, the chances that low pressure will lead to a flat increase. The most typical type of flat tire that occurs using clinchers at low pressure is the pinch flat. If you hit a rock, curb or other impediment on a 'cross course with low pressure, the rim will bottom out and pinch the tube between the impediment and the rim, rupturing the tube. This is why most cyclocross racers prefer tubular (or sewn-up) tires, a tire in which the tube is sewn into a casing and needs to be glued to the rim of the wheel. The advantage of the tubular is that it can be ridden at extremely low tire pressures, sometimes as low as 20 pounds PSI. At these low pressures, the tread and sidewalls of a tubular tire are able to mold themselves to the terrain allowing for greater surface area to contact the ground. This, in turn, means that you can ride turns faster and travel across the surface without bouncing, which is inefficient and wastes energy.

The disadvantage of the tubular is that it is another set of wheels you must acquire that will be exclusively cyclocross wheels. Unlike clincher wheels, tubular tires cannot be swapped on a whim. Once they are glued, you want them to stay glued until you get a puncture or decide to remove them.

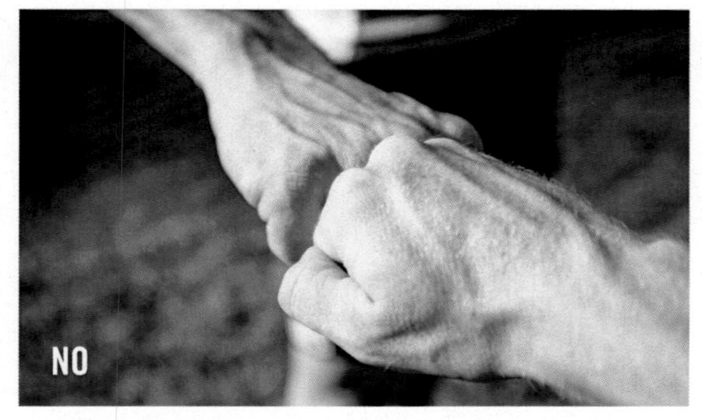

Proper technique for performing the cyclocross handshake.

Continue riding your first warm-up lap at a moderate pace, figuring out the best lines to take as you work your way around the course. As you are doing this, also pay attention to your tire pressure. A common mistake many new racers make is to over-inflate their tires. This is not a road race. You don't want your tires to be rock solid. In fact, the tire should be deflated to the point that you can depress the top of the tire so much you almost bottom out the tire on the rim. This rule, however, is rider-size dependent. Somebody who weighs 200 pounds will need more pressure than somebody weighing 130 lbs. How much the tire can be squeezed, also called the "cyclocross handshake," will vary.

Running low tire pressure allows the tire to better grip the ground. This improves your handling and also makes it possible to ride hills with loose dirt without having the tire spin or skip. One rule of thumb veteran racers use when running tubulars is that if you are bottoming out your tire (having the rim contact the ground) one time per lap, your pressure is pretty much dialed in. If you are bottoming out more than one time, conventional wisdom is to add more air until you reach that one-time limit. During your practice laps, play around with different tire pressures. Go too low one lap and too high the next. This way you will learn what different pressures feel like and what works best for you. Another good idea is to keep a tire journal in which you jot down the tire selection, tire pressure, conditions and any notes that might help you in the next race.

The final items you should concentrate on during your warm-up lap are the obstacles. The barriers, run-ups, sand, mud or any other special feature that forces you off your bike or calls upon special riding skill, such as riding through sand or mud, to complete. This is another area where, if you have time, you should ride the feature several times. Again, it's okay to duck under the tape and practice the section again. Just make sure you look behind you before getting back on the course so that you don't get in anybody's way, and don't go backwards on the course or otherwise block the other riders trying to pre-ride. There is nothing worse than crashing before the race begins. When previewing and practicing these sections, start off at an easy pace and then try a couple run-throughs at race pace just so you know what it's going to feel like at speed. This is a good practice to follow for any of the sections you decide to ride more than once. You will be surprised at how your approach and line changes the faster you go.

While you are riding the course also keep in mind the terrain and conditions. If you have multiple sets of wheels, these factors are going to help decide if you are going to ride a wet conditions tire or a dry conditions tire or a mix of the two. If you have time to do a second warm-up lap, it may be worthwhile changing up tires to see if you are more comfortable on a different set up. Riding different types of tires in practice is another great habit to get into. If you practice with other people, swap out wheels to get an idea of what is out there. Just make sure your drivetrains are compatible before trading with a friend.

ALL CONDITIONS TIRES

The name of this type of tire tread says it all. You can use this one in any condition a 'cross course will throw at you. The most common tread pattern out there is one that will have chevrons in the middle and some type of knob on the side that will allow you to corner in dry conditions as well as in the mud.

FILE TREAD TIRES

These tires are generally used for dry conditions. They have a diamond pattern down the middle of the tread for speed and a tall side-knob for grip going around the corner. You would typically only use this type of tread on a course that is all grass and dry or one that is dry and dusty.

MUD TIRES

As the name suggests, this tire tread is meant for the mud. Mud tires have tall widely-spaced knobs throughout the tread that allow the tire to grip the ground as well as shed accumulated mud while the tire rotates. You can run this type of tread on a dry course, but expect your speed to be slower since the tread grips the ground so well.

Once you finish your warm-up lap, ride over to registration and pick up your race number. Often, registration closes 30 minutes before a race begins, so if you race at 10:00 a.m., you must pick up your number no later than 9:30 a.m. Also remember that registering for a race and signing in are two separate steps that every racer must complete. Just because you registered on-line for the race does not mean you are automatically checked in. You still must go to the on-site registration, sign in and receive your number. If you do not, you will not be allowed to race.

Depending on how close you are to race time, the best time to have your last bit of solid food may be while you are waiting to register or immediately after that. This could be an energy bar or a homemade rice cake, but watch the sugar intake. Too much could cause you to get stomach cramps, known in the sport as "'cross gut." Also take a bottle of water or drink mix with you to registration. Staying hydrated before your race is important if you want to perform your best.

Jeremy Powers stops drinking an hour before the race and starts again with 15 minutes to go. Keep in mind, however, that if you race in hot weather it's a good idea to keep drinking right up until the start. A good place to start is to drink a 5-7% carbohydrate (CHO) mix to replace the sugar you burn in pre-ride and warm-up.

After you register and eat, the race in progress will be winding down. If your race is next, it's time to take care of your final preparations and start heading to the start area. If you are not racing next, there is still time to get in a second warm-up lap. This is also a good time to take that last trip to the porta-potty.

Number Pinning

In the race packet you pick up from registration will be your race number. If you've never pinned a number before here's what you do:

- Before leaving registration make sure to ask on which side of the jersey the number should be placed. This is important. If you have your number on the wrong side, the officials will not be able to see it when you ride through the finish line and you will not be scored.
- Pick up eight safety pins from the registration table. Do not crumple or fold your number. That veteran rider you have shadowed since arriving at the race may tell you that crumpling your number into a ball or folding it ensures a better adhesion to the jersey. Before deciding to follow suit, know that folding and crumpling numbers is against USA Cycling rules and your crumpling may result in a warning from an official.
- Most race numbers have little holes in each corner. Whatever these holes may be for—best guess is running races—they are not for pinning your number to your jersey. Using these holes allows for the number to flap around too much.
- Instead use one pin diagonally at each corner, and a pin running parallel to each edge of the number.

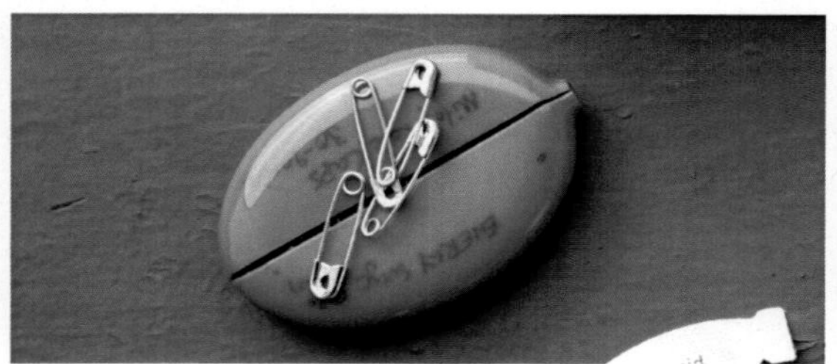

PINNING TIPS

- The best strategy for pinning the number if you are solo, is to lay your jersey or skinsuit out on your car, stretch the jersey, pin the number, try on your skinsuit or jersey and then readjust the pins to ensure the number is flat and taut.
- You can also sit, place the jersey with the left armhole over your left knee and the right armhole over your right knee. Open up your knees and stretch the jersey. Then start pinning the number to the appropriate side of the skinsuit or jersey. You can also put your jersey or skinsuit over the steering wheel of the car. This stretches the fabric and keeps you from pinning the front to the back of the skinsuit or jersey.
- Make sure that your number is not pinned upside down or on the wrong side.
- If you have a friend or significant other, they can pin you while you have your jersey or skinsuit already on. To do this bend over as if you are riding in the drops while your helper pins you. This will ensure that your number is flat and readable while passing the judges at the finish line.
- Another popular method for attaching numbers to jerseys is to apply spray-on glue to the back of the number. This method results in a clean and smooth application of the number but may get you a warning from officials unless you use safety pins, too. Glue alone is against USA Cycling rules. Be forewarned that using glue also results in a sticky mess on your jersey and skinsuit that may discolor the fabric.
- As you are cleaning up after your race, unpin your number and either return your pins to the organizer, or save them for use at your next race. A good trick is to buy or find an inexpensive rubber change purse. These are perfect for storing pins. Then just toss it in your gear bag.

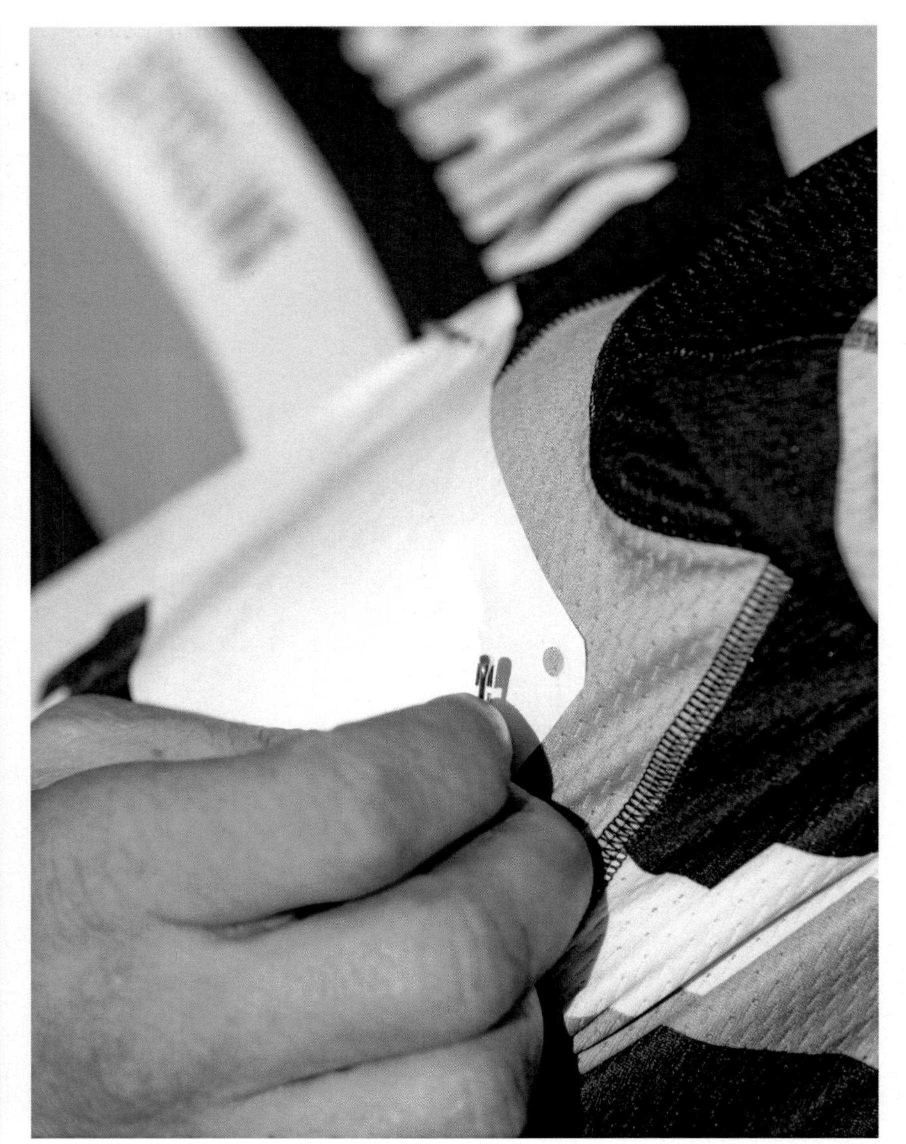

Find The Start

At some time during your pre-race routine you need to make a note of the starting grid's location. At some races there is a prologue section to the course, a long straight strip that is used only for the start. The prologue may not be near the finish line and not visible when you are doing your course recon. You need to scout out where it is or ask an official, so you are not caught searching for the start moments before the whistle. It is good practice to watch the start of a race before yours to see how the field sorts out. If possible, include the start in your pre-race recon laps.

Time permitting, also take a moment to inspect the start area. Note if it is on grass, gravel or pavement; if it is flat, downhill, or uphill; if there is a long straight, a tight turn or a major feature in the first few hundred meters. All of these factors will help you decide which side of the grid to line up on, how to approach the start, and what gear to be in.

Second Warm Up Lap

The second time out on the course should be a hot lap, at race speed and on the lines you picked during your first lap. It's still okay to go back and take tricky sections multiple times but you want to keep the pace up throughout this lap. Pay close attention to any terrain changes. A course changes throughout the day as hundreds of riders race multiple laps each. As the sun rises throughout the day, it can make a wet course tacky or a frozen course wet. You want to revisit your lines and also the sections you may want to run instead of ride. A section that may have been rideable earlier in the day could have eroded to a point that running is faster. Also keep in mind that a section that may be rideable when you are by yourself may be faster to run with traffic around you.

As you did on your first lap, watch what other people are doing in each section and weigh that into your decision. Also, watch the race in progress before you hit the course for your second warm-up lap. See what those riders are doing in the challenging sections of the course.

If this second lap is your final lap, ride it at race speeds to ensure that you are prepared to go when the whistle blows. Time permitting, try to do three or even as many as five warm-up laps on the course. If you are able to do more than two, adjust your efforts so that you do not go too hard. Keep that last lap as your race pace lap.

The optimal warm-up for many racers is to do some hard efforts to get the body ready for the race, and your muscles loose and primed. You want to activate your systems before you get into the race as well as making sure you know how sections of the course ride at race speeds. Go hard enough on parts of this lap that you are left out of breath. This will open your legs and lungs and have you prepared to race.

Placing your bike in a trainer for a final warm-up is another option. If the conditions are nasty, staying under a tent and keeping dry may be better than trying to ride the course. If going this route, you should consider packing a wheel with a road tire on it. Swapping out your 'cross wheel for a road wheel will make riding the trainer a quieter and less bumpy experience.

It's good to have a structured trainer warm-up planned to help activate your systems before the race start. Make sure that you have enough time to complete a longer trainer workout and that it does not come at the expense of a careful course inspection. For most racers in their first few seasons of 'cross, the biggest factor for success is simply avoiding mistakes. Getting more laps on the course—when you can try different lines and practice difficult sections—is one of the best ways to avoid mistakes.

If it is muddy, make sure you have the time to clean off the bike before your race begins. You do not want to head to the start line with a bike that is loaded down with extra weight and difficult to shift. If you do not have the time or means to clean your bike before the race, it may be best to skip the warm-up lap. Warm up on a trainer and be prepared to figure out the conditions as you go. Most likely, many of your competitors will have made the same decision.

If you decide not to do additional warm-up laps or if you still have time left after that lap is complete, you still want to keep warm. If the venue has rideable roads, continuing your warm-up on the road is a good option. Just make sure you give yourself enough time to get back to the start area.

SHIMANO
NEDERLAND
Rabobank

Depending on the temperature and conditions, you can roll up to the line with tights, rain pants, jacket, or leg/arm warmers. If you have teammates that are racing before or after you, ask them if they will collect your excess clothing from you. That way you can take that clothing off as close to your start time as you can so you stay warm and dry up until the last moment before the start. If it is raining and you don't have someone to collect your clothing, bring a plastic garbage bag and put your excess clothing in that at the start line so you have dry clothes when you finish your race.

Where's Your Head At?

Staging for a 'cross race can be nerve-wracking. Your mind may race, worrying about your preparation, equipment choices, and how you stack up to your competition. Try to calm your mind, as those are all aspects that are in the past, and focus on the immediate task ahead of you: a successful race start and executing your race plan. Take your thoughts inward, breathe deep, and envision the major course features you have inspected during your course inspection and warm-up. Then clear your mind, trust your preparations and mentally prepare to push yourself to the limit.

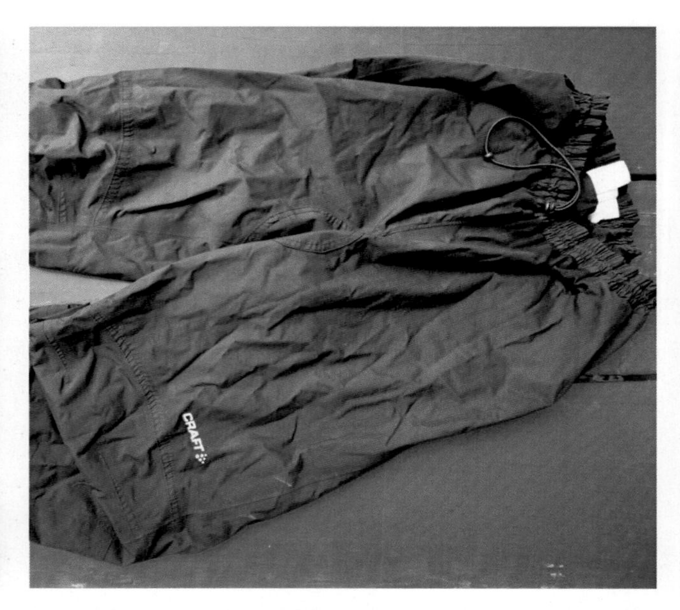

Final Preparations

- Following your warm-up, make your way to the start area to watch the start of the next race. Pay particular attention to any places that bottleneck and take note of which side of the pack seems to get around it best. Mentally log this information to inform your choice of starting grid location during staging. Often times, the fastest starting grid location is counter-intuitive based on where the bottlenecks occur in the first 1-2 minutes of the race.
- Make sure you are at the staging area with plenty of time before the start. A good rule of thumb is to be at the staging area no later than 15 minutes before the start of your race. Time your warm-up and any last-minute bathroom stops so you are finishing up and heading to the start at this time.
- If the starting area is open, do a couple of practice starts. During these practice starts, pick out lines on both sides of the course. If you are stuck in traffic and need to change course at the start, you will still have a good idea about where you want to go. Use your practice starts from earlier to pick the correct gear.

In the beginner category—also called category 5 for men, category 4 for women or category C—there may not be call-ups. Check the race or series rules to make sure. A call-up is reserved for series leaders or racers who the organizer wishes to recognize with a starting position at the front of the grid. Racers are normally instructed to wait in a staging area, which is sometimes called the bullpen. The official will then call up racers one by one to populate the starting grid. The first 16 to 24 riders are typically called up. After call-ups, staging is usually by promoter or series discretion. In many instances, the remaining spots are first-come-first-staged, by an online service such as Crossresults.com or series standings, or by registration number.

To avoid the scrum, when racers are released en masse and allowed to choose their own starting spot, many organizers have started to pre-populate the starting grid. In other words, they have determined where you will be staged before race day and assigned you a race number that corresponds to your starting position. So if you have race number 18, for example, and each row has eight spots, you will be the second rider in the third row.

- Be sure to wear tights, jacket or other weather appropriate clothing for your wait in the staging area. You do not want to get cold standing on the line, which in a worst-case scenario could be 20 minutes or longer. Be prepared.
- Put your water bottle in your jersey pocket or stick it down the back of your skinsuit along with a gel. Once you get to staging, continue to drink and if it's part of your nutrition strategy don't forget to ingest the gel.
- It's a good practice to have somebody double-check at the start that your number is on the correct side and not upside down.

THE STANDARD STARTING GRID

- **Eight vertical lanes marked with chalk or tape.**
- **Horizontal lines may be added to the grid so that rows are easily distinguished.**
- **Course tape and stakes line the sides of the starting grid to prevent riders from "sneaking up" the sides before the whistle blows.**
- **For many races that pre-populate the starting grid according to race number, the organizers will include row signs that let riders know what bib numbers are in each row. For instance, the signs will say Row 1 Nos. 1-8, Row 2 Nos. 9-16, etc. This practice is an orderly way to get everybody lined up quickly without an official having to call out everybody in the field by name.**

RACE REGISTRATION

Be forewarned that in most race series, if you register the day of the race, you will start near the back of the field. This is even true for racers who have earned a call-up. Race organizers want everybody to pre-register for races. It saves time on race day and ensures races will stay on schedule.

Staging

- The chief referee or race organizer will call up riders from the bullpen or riders will be expected to find their correct row.
- The officials will make sure everybody is lined up in the right spot and race numbers are attached on the correct side of the body and not upside down.
- The officials will also check to see that nobody has saddle bags, lights or other attachments to their bike that they believe may cause a safety hazard. Depending on the official, this may include cameras attached to the bike or racer.
- Once the racers are staged, the promoter may say a few quick announcements. At this point you should have removed all of the clothing you will not be racing in and handed it to a friend, significant other or teammate on the sideline.
- If nobody is available for this hand off, bring a plastic bag to the start line and store your clothes and water bottle in that bag and toss it to the side. This is most important if race conditions are rainy or cold. Having dry, warm clothes available post-race is something you will want.
- Try to stage behind riders that you know have good technique, start well and pick good lines (known quantities).
- Stage on the side that gets through the first feature fastest in earlier races

The Start

After everyone is staged, the official will give last-minute instructions about the course, scoring or other items of note. After the announcements have concluded, the official will inform the racers to start on the whistle. In some regions the official will give a 30-second warning. In others, the official will simply blow the whistle or fire the gun and the race will start. At this point, you should be taking deep breaths and preparing for the whistle. This is not a good time to chat with friends and neighbors in the start grid—this is "business time." You want to pay attention to the instructions from the official and be prepared when the 30 second warning is given.

THE SECRET START

With 30 seconds to go, the official in most regions will announce to the field that the whistle will sound anytime within the next half-minute. Not knowing when the whistle will blow or the gun will fire in that timeframe is known as the "secret start." Some officials may also do the "double-secret-start" in which they combat the unfair advantage afforded the front of the field who can see the official preparing to blow the whistle. After giving the 30-second warning, the official starts walking down the side of the staging area towards the back of the field. At some point during this move to the back of the grid, the official will blow the whistle or fire the gun. From this rear-guard position, the front of the field is unable to key in to when exactly the whistle will sound, making the start significantly fairer.

THE NOT-SO-SECRET START

In some areas, officials stand in front of the field and count down the start like they're sending a rocket into space. They start counting backwards from 10 and blow the whistle or fire the gun after "one." The problem with this method is that the whole field knows exactly when the start will happen. In this scenario, the field will often jump the gun or whistle by a couple beats. With large fields it is next to impossible to call everybody back if the front of the pack leaves early. In most races that start with a countdown, if you're not 20 meters up the road by the time the whistle blows, you're most likely already behind the field. Some areas will still occasionally use the "Le Mans" start, still popular at some mountain bike events, where riders run to their bikes. If you live in one of these areas, push promoters for proper 'cross starts.

The Sorting

Every course has a bottleneck—a spot where the field of racers will slow to a crawl because not everybody will be able to smoothly fit through part of the course. It could be the first turn or some other tricky section of the course on the first lap, but it will inevitably happen. If you have had the opportunity to watch earlier racers, you should already know where the slowdown will occur. Your goal should be to get out in front of the bottleneck. Usually the first 10-15 riders will squeeze through the trouble section without having to slow down. If you are in that front group you are going to gain seconds over the field without having to expend unnecessary energy.

If you can't move up safely—for example, you staged 80th—and you get caught in the bottleneck, stay within yourself and save your matches for later in the race. The leaders may put some distance on you, but don't think that you need to make up the time you lost all at once. If you spend a lot of energy right after a bottleneck to catch up with the lead group, chances are you will eventually drift back from that group. The front riders will likely be fresher than you and you won't have the opportunity to properly recover after catching them. Instead, stay within yourself and ride as hard as you can without going into the red. Eventually the pace of that front pack is going to stabilize and, if you have the strength to do so, you can start making your way back to the front.

The better strategy is to work hard at the start and make sure you are up near the front. There is nothing wrong with being aggressive and moving up several positions right off the line. Just be smart and safe. Don't swerve abruptly for no reason, run into other riders or get caught in a spot where you have to grab a handful of brakes. What is perhaps most important is to protect your front wheel. That means keep riders in front of you from hitting it, but also don't run into things like other riders, course stakes or tape. You'll probably stay upright if someone runs into you from the side or back, but things hitting your front wheel often lead to crashes. Don't worry—the people behind you are responsible for their own front wheels. Also, if the race comes to a standstill consider dismounting and running around the bottleneck, passing those who are standing still, straddling their bikes.

If the opportunity exists to make a move early, it's a great time to do so. Prologue sections of courses are sometimes the widest and straightest sections. Blasting to the front at this point in the race and then settling in somewhere in the top 20 is going to have you in a good position for the race. As you gain more experience, start trying to move up. Get in the top 15 at the start, and then the top 10.

Once you are at the front, the goal is to hang on. This is where the mental side of racing comes in to play. If you are in the correct category and racing against people close to your skill and fitness level, the first laps of a race at the front hurt. Your body is at the limit and your brain is screaming at you to take the foot off the gas and ride at a more reasonable pace. The key is to try and ignore the pain as long as possible and keep with the faster group. Eventually your body may give up and you will lose spots. This is acceptable. Regroup and start riding the fastest pace you can. For your next race, come back and try to stay on the group a little longer. If you push yourself like this, by the end of the season you may find that staying with the "fast group" is much easier and you are able to animate the action rather than just hang on.

A typical early race bottleneck.

RACE STRATEGY

As discussed at the beginning of this book, cyclocross is all about battles. You may be battling for the win or a podium spot, but you also may be battling for top 30 or to beat your nemesis who always gets the better of you. A sound race strategy can help you win the battle. For tactical purposes, a cyclocross race can be divided into three parts: the start, the middle laps, and the finish. You need to have a strategy for each of these phases.

When you are waiting to be staged, look around at your competition. If you know who you are racing against and what kind of starter different racers are, keep that in mind as you find your spot on the grid. If the race is staged row by row instead of a scrum start, you will be told your starting row. But you usually are able to choose any open slots in that row. Take a look at the row ahead of you and try to line up behind somebody you know is a strong starter. Likewise, avoid the folks who you know are poor starters or who have a hard time avoiding crashes.

If the podium is your realistic goal, the optimal place to be after the start is in the first five spots. Racers who slot in anywhere from first to tenth place usually have a good shot of winning the race or securing a podium spot. After that, moving to the front of a race becomes more difficult. Not impossible, but really difficult for most racers. If you have a bad start or get caught behind a crash, working your way through the field to make sure that are top five by the end of the first lap is a good first goal for the race.

If your race goal isn't to win races, but rather to consistently improve your results, work hard at the start to secure a good position as far up in the pack as you can, and settle in for the race. As the adage goes, "the most important sprint in cyclocross is at the start, not the end."

Being in first place after the start—also known as "winning the holeshot"—is an impressive feat, but it may not always be the best tactical move. If you can do this, it means you are most likely a strong sprinter. However, the race has just begun and you don't want to burn all your matches in the first 30 seconds. If you are consistently winning the holeshot but fading after a lap or two, ease off a bit and settle into a group that pushes you, but won't drop you. This may mean as little as settling for fifth place instead of first after the start. Save that monster sprint for the end.

After the start, the field will usually stay together until the first tricky turn or obstacle on the course. Knowing where this spot could potentially be is important for your start strategy. If you know a certain spot is going to be difficult, make sure that you are in front of or close to your competition, so if you do lose time you can hopefully make it up. The first group of riders will most likely make it through this section without slowing down. The rest of the field, however, will be forced to slow down and the separation between riders will begin to appear. The ensuing chaos usually lasts only for a couple minutes at most. After that, racers settle in. By no means does the race get easier, but a rhythm and consistency of effort is established. This is where the second phase of the race begins. It's time to take stock of the race situation, assess the group you are in and determine if you can move up to a group farther up the road.

You're in your group, so what now? Unlike road racing, drafting riders in cyclocross has its pitfalls. Unless there is a long, straight, smooth section on the course, drafting is risky. If the rider in front of you crashes, bobbles or brakes harder than expected, you will, at the very least, lose momentum, and, at worst, you may end up crashing and abandoning the race. Give the racer in front of you enough room so that (A) he is not dictating your lines or speed and (B) you can get around the rider without slowing down or crashing if that rider makes a mistake.

Similar to road racing, accelerating out of corners can yield great gains in cyclocross, especially in the lower fields where riders have not learned this skill. When you come into a tricky corner that requires you to coast rather than pedal through it, don't expend energy at that point. Instead, wait until you begin to exit the turn and expend that saved energy by accelerating out of the corner. Similarly, on a downhill you sometimes coast and don't expend energy for a couple of seconds. Trade off those seconds of recovery by accelerating as soon as you can. The goal is to match every savings of energy with an expenditure of energy. It's no exaggeration to say that bicycle racing is primarily about smart energy management.

Likewise, you should treat every climb like it is a little bit longer than it actually is. In other words, keep pedaling hard even after you crest the top of the hill. A tendency for many new racers is to stop pedaling right at the top of the climb in an effort to recover. If you continue to hammer through and over the peak, you will get up to speed faster and have more momentum once the terrain flattens.

As you ride with your group, start taking mental notes about the riders with you and how you stack up against them. Be analytical about it. Is the group going at your race pace or are you not giving full effort for fear of going off the front and blowing up? It's always easier to ride in a group than attack it, but if you don't feel like you're producing a race pace effort (i.e. you aren't hitting the threshold of your fitness and you find yourself doing a lot of coasting) it's time to be aggressive (but safe) and get out in front. At that point your next objective is to find your optimal race pace and start reeling in the next group in front of you.

If you believe that the group you are racing with is a group that is at your level, take a look at the other racers and note how they perform on different parts of the course. Someone in your group may corner better than you, but you may have more fitness than they do. Maybe you are a faster runner but you always lose ground on rideable climbs. Figure out where you are putting time into the racer chasing you—or the one whom you're chasing—and where that person is making up ground.

Once you have a good read on everybody, it's time to formulate a plan. The foundation of that plan is the following: know what your strengths and weaknesses are so that you can use them to your advantage. If you are faster through a section, get out in front and make those behind you work harder. If you are weaker in a section, also get out in front and control the speed of those behind you. For instance, if you notice you are always losing ground over the planks, get to the front of your group and take the barriers first. This will disrupt the rhythm of those behind you and minimize your losses.

Although you are attacking these sections, the attacks are not necessarily ones in which you give it everything you have. They are more like surges that give you advantages you can use to exploit your competition. Maximizing your technical proficiency not only provides you more areas where you can attack the course, it also limits where the competition can attack you.

Going all out to exploit someone's weakness early in the race is usually not a smart tactic, especially if that person is otherwise as strong a racer as you. If exploiting a weakness does not cause you to expend much energy—such as being faster in corners—go for it. But if you need to put in a big effort, it may be better to keep that card in your hand until later in the race, when there is no chance for your competition to recover. Patience is key here. For instance, if you know that you are faster in the corners than your competitors, don't go all out every time. Hold back until the end of the race and then attack.

Likewise, if you are a gifted runner, don't show this card right away. For most bike racers, running hard spikes their heart rate. It is common in cyclocross that many racers run slower for fear that they will blow up. If running is your strength, pick the right time to exploit it. For instance, pick a spot that everybody is riding but you know you can run faster. Ride with the group through this section until the lap you have planned your attack. Get off and run and leave them all behind.

And this brings us to the final third of the race. The last lap(s). As much as making your winning move is important on these final laps, the best strategy for a race may be making no move at all. If you are racing in tricky conditions, experimenting on the final laps with a new line or riding something you've run the rest of the race can be costly. Especially if the race is muddy.

RACE LOG

After your race, jot down your thoughts about the race in a notebook. Include course conditions, tire selection and pressure, clothing worn and how your race went. Also include notes about the people you raced against in your group: what were their strengths, where were they putting in gaps on you, when did you have to expend extra energy to keep up with them, and what technical sections gave them trouble. This is information you can use in the next race, especially if you will be racing against the same competition week after week.

If you are confident that you can race aggressively, it's time to put your race plan into action. Keep in mind that by putting in an attack you will likely be navigating sections of the course at a higher rate of speed than you have throughout the race. This means you have to adjust the lines you take, where you brake, and how quickly you approach obstacles. Also be aware that some sections can only be ridden at a certain speed. Attacking these spots with "speed limits" can mute your attack.

Once you make the initial move, the real work begins. Just being faster in one short section is not going to make a difference if you do not commit to the attack. That means going into the red, or burning a match. You need to stretch that attack out for another 10, 15 or even 30 seconds to make it stick. Everybody is hurting late in the race. You need to win the psychological battle by getting enough distance between you and your competitors that they do not think chasing is worth the effort. If you attack and then sit up while still in view of the group you left, your competitors will think catching up is possible and start chasing in earnest. Use the corners or switchbacks to scope out where your competition is so that you do not have to slow down to check behind you. Most of all, going 100% in the closing minutes of a race is the time to concentrate the hardest on performing technical skills flawlessly. The combination of maximal exertion and the excitement of being on the attack are a great recipe for forgetting the basics and making mistakes.

If your strategy is to not attack in the last laps but instead to wait until the finishing stretch to make your move, knowing how the course ends is crucial. Don't concentrate only on the final stretch. Instead, you want to consider the final few turns of a course and the last tricky obstacle. These are the points you need to study. In most cross races, being first out of the last technical section is the winning move.

So how are you going to come out of the section before that in a position to win? Do you need to take a different line? Do you have a card to play that will give you an advantage over your group? Do you just need to get to that section before the other guys because you can't ride it as well and want to neutralize that advantage? Can you sprint into that section ahead of your competition? These are all scenarios you should be thinking about during your course recon. This is not something that only the podium finishers need to keep in mind. Every spot counts in 'cross and winning moves are not exclusive to the top three.

Knowing what type of rider you are by identifying your strengths and weaknesses is going to go a long way in determining how you play this final part of the race. If you're a sprinter or a strong road racer you probably want to conserve your energy as long as possible and try to sprint for the win. Conversely, if you're a technically gifted rider who loses ground on the straights, getting a gap a bit earlier with a better line through the mud or around a corner will force the other guys to chase a little harder. If you force them to burn a match before the end, your chances in a sprint increase over guys who are naturally stronger finishers.

Learning how to make a successful winning move is important. Equally important is learning how to refocus if the move doesn't work. Part of being a tactically sound racer is the ability to hit the reset button if something goes wrong. Everybody who races at some point will drop a chain, crash in a corner, get cut off or bobble in the mud. If you are able to quickly put the setback behind you and continue to race, the sport is much more fun and your results will improve. At some point during your season bad luck will find you. When it does, and you see your group going up the road without you, don't panic. Remember your plan, your fundamentals and your race goals, then get back to it. Time lost is not going to be gained back all at once. Race hard, learn from your mistakes and look forward to doing it again next week.

The corners of a cyclocross course can be used as a strategic advantage. If you are entering a corner first, you can control how the person behind you rides. You do not want to ride dangerously or abandon the smooth line you found, but by riding tape to tape, you can effectively keep your momentum while fending against passes and forcing competitors to change course.

PASSING DRILLS (REQUIRES 2 OR MORE RIDERS):

Set up an oval course with two 180-degree turns with cones, or water bottles or whatever you have available. Be sure to not only mark the inside of the turn, but put cones on the exit of the turns as well to mark the limit of how wide you can turn.

Start with the first rider taking a normal arc through the turn, while the other rider(s) follow. Next have the other rider(s) practice an inside-out pass in which they start a bit wider than the first rider, then dive inside of the first rider and accelerate out of the turn. This will teach the first rider to hold his or her line as another rider encroaches, and will teach the other rider(s) how to execute an outside-in pass. In the beginning, do not have the first rider defend the line or accelerate to keep the other rider(s) from executing the pass. Next, have the riders swap roles. Invariably, this will progress to the next phase, which is for the first rider to defend the line and keep the speed up. This competitive progression is the perfect progression for the drill.

Next, repeat the drill by executing an inside-out pass in which the trailing rider(s) initiates the turn on the inside of the first rider and naturally pushes the first rider to the outer edge of the turn (or in the tape on a race course). Be careful on this drill, as it has a higher probability of contact, and if you get too competitive it can result in some rather aggressive shoulder barges.

Next, mix the drill up with the trailing rider(s) working on setting up the pass, then executing it safely, using either of the passing techniques. Often, this may require setting up the pass over several turns. The leading rider will try to protect the line and either set up outside or inside, which allows the trailing rider(s) to take the opposite entry into the turn. Keep it safe, but have fun and experiment.

A variant to this drill is to do it using the Peanut Drill setup, which means more opportunities to pass in different situations.

THE PITS

In a race run under USA Cycling rules, a course must have an equipment pit, a part of the circuit where riders can change wheels or bicycles. Courses are supposed to have two pit areas for riders to use and they are not to be located on stony, gravel or downhill stretches. In many instances, one pit will be in a place that can be accessed from two spots on the course. This type of pit is known as a double pit or double-sided pit. A double pit is required for championships and recommended for other events sanctioned by USA Cycling.

The pit area includes a pit box area where bikes, wheels and tools are stored, and a pit lane where bike and wheel exchanges are made. At the pro level, a rider will have a two-person crew working in the pit. This crew is responsible for cleaning, adjusting and repairing bikes between laps and having a race-ready bike available for the rider when they come through the pit for an exchange. Most pros place one or more bikes in the pit boxes so they can exchange them throughout the race. In a muddy race, racers may exchange bikes every half lap. This could mean making 20 bike changes throughout a single race.

At the amateur level, many racers do not have a pit bike. A common option is to place a spare set of wheels in the pit so that you have it available during your race, if you get a flat or damage a wheel. Also, placing a tool set or even just a multi-tool in the pit in case you have a mechanical is a good plan.

The USA Cycling rulebook states: "A rider may use the pit lane only to change a bicycle or wheel." (Rule 4C1). At first glance, this looks like it excludes any other repairs or going through the pit without changing your bike or wheel. Shawn Farrell, USA Cycling technical director, supplied the following explanation: "A rider can stop in a pit to make repairs to his bike. He does not need to change a bike or a wheel, and nowadays, feed."

Riders are also allowed to ride through the pit lane without receiving any assistance if they unclip and put a foot down in the pit lane. Farrell explained that "the one foot down rule is not in writing anywhere, but is a typical thing that we do at all levels, including UCI, if a rider enters a pit and does not stop for anything."

Not doing any of these things could result in a rider being disqualified from the race and not being placed in the results.

If you are just starting out, having a second set of wheels or a pit bike may not be an option, but you can still be prepared by staging some tools in the pit in case you need to make a mid-race adjustment. If you are racing on a team, you may have some friends racing in other categories that will let you use their spare wheels, or even their bike. Regardless, to the uninitiated the pits can seem like a chaotic and intimidating area. Rest assured that, while it is indeed chaotic at times, there is a method to the madness. Understanding what is going on will help you use this vital resource that is unique to cyclocross.

Spare Bike vs. Spare Wheels

The decision comes down to cost, logistics and convenience. A pit bike is always going to be a better option. It allows you to have a spare bike to use if something happens to your "A" bike in warm ups. It allows you to warm up in muddy conditions with your "B" bike while keeping the "A" bike race ready. If you have somebody working your pit for you, they can start cleaning that bike while you make your way down to the start. The pit bike is also faster to change during a race. Even if you don't have a pit person, grabbing a pit bike after a mechanical or flat is much quicker than having to change wheels or make repairs.

During a muddy race, a big advantage can be gained by riding a clean bike. Your bike can gain several pounds per lap during a muddy race. Having a pit person available to clean the mud off your pitted bike, and exchanging every lap (or half lap), will shave time off of your result. Even if you don't have a pit person, changing bikes halfway through the race or with two laps to go, and racing that important last portion of the race on a lighter, faster bike will make a difference.

Mud is destructive. If it is thick or frozen, it gets clogged in the bike's drivetrain and can cause catastrophic mechanicals. Having a rear derailleur rip off the bike is not an uncommon result in a muddy race. Keeping your bike(s) as clean as possible during a race is the best way to prevent these types of mishaps.

Spare Wheels

Spare wheels are better than nothing. They are a less expensive option and easier to pack if you are carpooling to a race. Having spare wheels allows you a different tread option, too. Assuming you have mud and dry tires on your wheels, you can figure out what works best for the race, and keep the others in the pit. And don't be afraid to experiment with mixing and matching. Having an aggressive (mud) tread in the front for cornering traction, and a faster tread in the rear for lower rolling resistance may be the right formula for your race conditions.

Pit Person

If you are on a team, there should be an understanding among members that you will work for each other in the pits. Not everyone will race in the same category. Pit for each other. It's part of how a team should work, you will see the race from a different perspective, and it's actually quite a bit of fun.

If you are not on a team, make friends. Also, if it is a muddy race, offer to pay someone to pit for you. $20 or even a six-pack of beer can go a long way.

It's not about the money, necessarily, but about the appreciation that someone is giving up their time to help you.

The first thing a pit person needs to know is where the pit is located and if power washers or a hose are available. If not, and it is a muddy race, be prepared to bring a bucket or three and as much water as you can carry. You can also invest in a portable power washer. Battery packs are available for these devices so they can be used almost anywhere.

Communication is key. Talk with your pit person before the race about what gear you want your bike in when you are exchanging, and if there are any special instructions on how to perform the exchange. If this is the first time working with a pit person, do a couple practice exchanges to make sure you are on the same page. While it should be understood that you'll want the right pedal at the 3 o'clock position for a fast remount, a non-cyclocross racer may not know that.

Once the race begins, communication is even more important. Don't be afraid to yell to—not at—your pit person or crew to let them know you are coming into the pit. Sometimes just a look in their direction and a briefly raised hand can accomplish that. Also, when exchanging bikes, let them know what is wrong. If it just needs to be cleaned, no words are necessary. But if you need more or less air in a tire, your brakes are rubbing or some other issue is happening, then clearly state that as you approach.
It really only makes sense to have a pit person if you have a spare bike. You won't save much time on a wheel change if you or somebody else does it. The benefit of a pit person is that they will take care of your spare bike and have it ready to exchange when you need it. When the next exchange happens, the pit person will make sure the bike is in the ideal gear and that the drive-side is at 3 o'clock so that you can drive down with your right leg and go.

The Exchange

When you come into the pit for an exchange, ride through the pit lane and dismount the same way you would for a standard carry, but don't lift your bike. You want to time your dismount so that you are a few steps away from your pit person who will be holding your spare bike with one hand by the saddle. As you get to the pit person, gently let go of your current bike and steer it to the right of the new bike. You want to be sure the old bike does not hook onto the new one you're taking. The pit person may or may not catch it with his or her free hand or your pit person may have made a friend in the pit who is catching your bike. Either way is fine. What is important is that once you release your current bike, continue running, place your hands on the tops of the handlebars of the new bike, take a couple steps with the bike and remount. As you get more proficient with pitting with a one-person pit crew, you can help your pit person out by guiding your dirty bike to the person's free hand, and they can help you out by giving your clean bike a subtle push so that you can maintain your momentum. A couple of practice exchanges in a clean area will help you and your pit person work out the kinks. Practice until your bike stays upright, you don't plunge your dirty bike into the gut of your pit person, and you smoothly transition to your clean bike. Your pit person will then take care of any issues you had with the bike you dropped off, including cleaning it, and getting it ready for the next exchange.

Remember there is a rule that a rider can take no more than three steps without a bicycle, so you want to discard the old bike close enough to the new one that only a few steps are required.

Two Person Pit Crew

If you are lucky enough to have two people working your pit, the exchange is much easier. After you dismount, you can release your current bike into the waiting hands of the first pit person. Take a step or two and grab the new bike from the second pit person who will be holding the bike from the right handlebar and seat. As you approach your bike, the pit person will give the bike a subtle push forward so your transition is smoother. By having a bike catcher, the second pit person can concentrate on making sure your new bike is steady and upright.

When working in the pits, be aware that you are not alone. Each person is working for a rider. When a race is muddy, the pit is a chaotic place. Concentration is key. Make sure you let everybody know when your rider is coming in so they will stay clear. In the same vein, stay out of the way when other riders enter the pit, never loiter or spectate in the pit, and especially not in the exchange lane.

ONE PERSON EXCHANGE

TWO PERSON EXCHANGE
50
Haymarket

50
Haymarket

50
Haymarket

50
Haymarket

Pit Tools

At minimum, have a multi-tool available in the pits. It should have several Allen wrench sizes, a Phillips and flathead screwdriver. If you do not have spare wheels, consider bringing a tire iron, spare tube, a tire boot and a pump. Also, bring chain lube—in a spray can is ideal—to help get drivetrain and cables working smoothly. If there is no bike-washing area provided, bring a bucket of water, an old water bottle that you don't mind getting dirty, a large scrub brush and a couple towels and rags. By quickly dipping the water bottle into the bucket and filling it up, you can make yourself a makeshift water jet to dislodge mud/dirt and rinse the bike.

PIT DRILL:

Using a moderately large open space, discuss the sequence of events with your pit crew (one or two people). Make sure to talk about the gearing of your pit bike, the ideal pedal location for the remount, and where the crew will hold your pit bike. Also, discuss how you will be handing off your bike to the crew. Remember not to skewer your pit crew with a high-speed ghost bike.

At first, start this drill at a slow speed and execute a standard dismount, then pass the bike off to your crew and receive your pit bike in full stride. After the first few attempts, swing back around to discuss any changes that you or your crew want to make. Then repeat the drill multiple times, slowly speeding up the pace of your entry.

This drill only takes five minutes to practice, but getting you and your pit crew on the same page is priceless—it can save countless seconds during each exchange.

CLOTHING

Everything discussed in this section is aimed at optimal performance—from skinsuits to proper shoes and everything in between. But not having this gear shouldn't stop you from racing. The hope is that, when you're starting out, you don't worry about most of it.

In time, when you are racing more, revisit this section and figure out the best gear to have. If you show up for your first race in baggy shorts, a t-shirt and a 15-year old mountain bike, that's fine. In the end it's about getting your bike to the starting line and getting hooked on the sport. Before you know it, you'll forget the time in your life when shaving your legs and slathering on embrocation wasn't a normal part of your daily routine. So what needs to be on the list? Let's start with essential clothing.

When reading through this section, you will notice a lot of redundancy. This is on purpose. Eventually you will want to have several options of all the gear you own. Cyclocross is a sport that is hard on equipment. You must have a backup plan.

Jerseys And Bibshorts

- A quality racing jersey is going to conform to your body, fit comfortably and wick moisture. If you are new to the sport, a jersey does not have to be expensive. Fit and comfort are more important than style.
- Cycling shorts have a padded chamois sewn on where you make contact with the saddle. Comfort and a snug fit are important when choosing shorts. (And NEVER wear underwear under your shorts, it defeats the purpose.)
- The bibshort—shorts with shoulder straps connected—are a difficult item for those new to cycling to comprehend. However, bibs are a great improvement over the traditional cycling short. Bibshorts do not have a waistband so they are more comfortable when in a racing position. They also will not sag, an important feature in cyclocross because it is all too easy to catch sagging fabric on the saddle during remounts. Even if you plan on racing in a skinsuit, you still should bring at least one jersey and bibshorts to the race to warm up in, and to have as a backup.
- If you are racing two days in a row, a third jersey/bib set is essential—especially if you don't have access to a washing machine.
- If it is a cool day, having a long-sleeved jersey to warm up in is a great option. It is also a nice item to wear over your skinsuit to carry a water bottle and keep you warm as you wait in the staging area for your race to begin. A thermal or waterproof jacket takes that to the next level on colder or rainy days.
- Having a jersey and bibshorts on hand as a backup plan is invaluable if you break a zipper or have some other wardrobe malfunction with your skinsuit.
- Bring a short-sleeved and long-sleeved jersey to the race. If you only own short-sleeved jerseys, arm warmers will also be essential.

Skinsuits

The skinsuit is something new racers look at with about as much suspicion as shaved legs. Do you need to wear one to race 'cross? Definitely not. But here's why you might consider it:

- In cyclocross you are calling on much more of your body to participate in the sport. In road racing, the upper body is more or less static while the legs do the work. In 'cross, you are on and off your bike, avoiding obstacles, tree branches, running, shouldering and wallowing in mud and muck. The last thing you want is for your jersey to get in the way. A skinsuit decreases the opportunity for objects to get stuck in your jersey and eliminates the need for you to rearrange your kit every time you get off your bike.
- Like the name implies, a skinsuit is like a second skin. There is no extra material flapping around, getting caught in the wind. This decreases resistance and may make you faster. Sure, how much faster it makes you is open to debate, but it's safe to say it isn't going to make you slower.
- Much like the summer is bikini season, cyclocross is skinsuit season. If ever there was an incentive for getting fit, shedding those extra pounds and looking your best, it's the prospect of donning the skinsuit come cyclocross season. There are no secrets when you are wearing a skinsuit.
- If you do not have a skinsuit, have at least two jerseys and bibshorts. If it is a hot day, or a rainy day, you will have a damp jersey after you are done warming up. Changing right before your race is a great way to feel fresh, dry and comfortable before the start.

SKINSUIT VARIATIONS

- **Even if the forecast is for warm or cool temperatures, if you own a long-sleeved and short-sleeved skinsuit, bring them both.**
- **If you can only afford one, the safe bet is probably a long-sleeved version. Skinsuit material is fairly thin and a long-sleeved one should be bearable in warmer temperatures. When the temperature does drop, you won't have to worry about arm-warmers falling down or getting stuck on your bike during carries.**
- **For really cold temperatures, many manufacturers also make fleece-lined skinsuits, and skinsuits that incorporate knickers. Before investing in these items, make sure you are going to need them. Wearing a base layer and knee warmers can serve the same purpose. If you aren't racing deep into the winter, buying a fleece-lined skinsuit could be overkill.**

Base Layer

Like many things in cycling the base layer is a personal choice.

- When it's cold out, different weight and sleeve length base layers allow you to dial in your comfort level while racing. Many times when you are warming up, a heavier base layer may feel comfortable, but by the time you hit the line, your core temperature may have risen to the point that the base layer is going to cause you to overheat during the race. It is a good idea to invest in several different types so that you are racing at the ideal temperature for your performance. Just keep in mind that it is best to show up to the line a bit chilly than too warm. You will warm up quickly as the race progresses.
- Another base layer option has a windproof front. This is a good choice for cold, windy days.
- Changing base layers after your warm up is another way to stay dry and comfortable in the starting grid before your race.
- The best-case scenario is to own sleeveless, short-sleeved and long-sleeved base layers of varying weights.

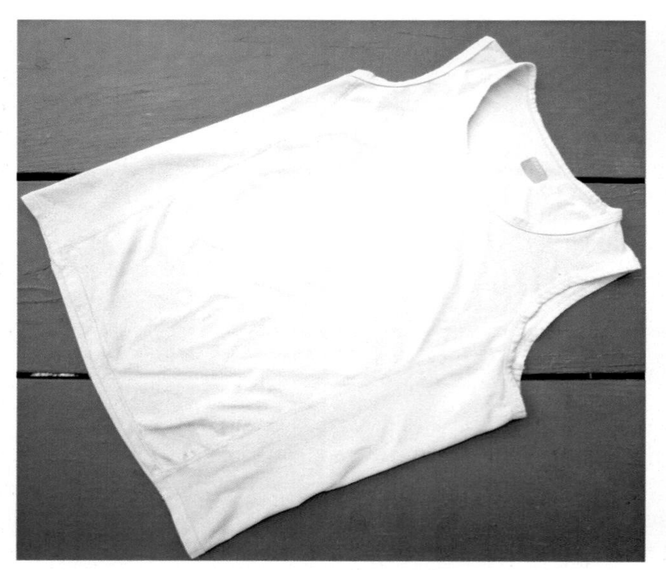

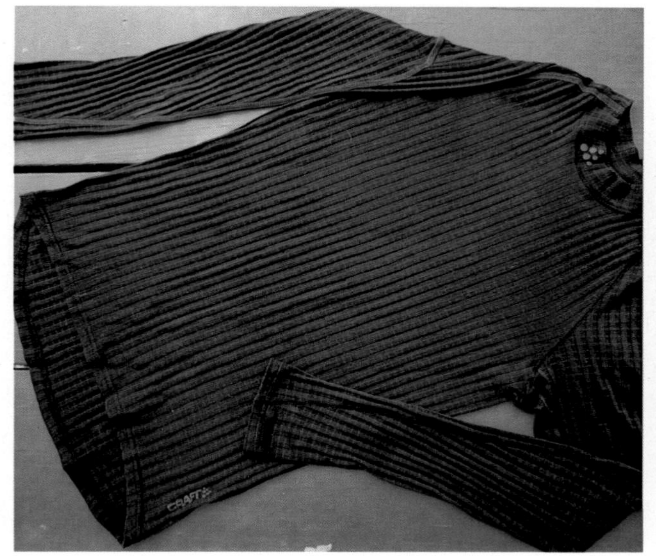

Socks

Like base layers, socks are a clothing item that comes under the personal preference designation. The two most popular sock types are wool and synthetic.

- Wool socks are usually made of merino wool and are relatively soft and thin. They offer some warmth and also are decent at wicking moisture.
- A thick wool sock may constrict blood flow, thereby feeling colder than a thin one, if your shoes are too tight.
- Synthetic socks are generally thinner than wool, which allows for you to get a snug shoe fit without constricting blood flow. Thin, breathable socks also prevent your feet from overheating during races. Many also include a measure of compression that may keep your feet from cramping.
- If you race in a UCI-sanctioned event, sock height matters. Tall socks—higher than the midpoint between the ankle and the knee—are not allowed, presumably to prevent the use of compression socks. If you race in a non-UCI race, wear whatever you like. In those races, it's mostly about style, unless you choose to wear a compression sock in the hopes of gaining an advantage—sometimes referred to as "sock doping."
- Cotton is not used for cycling clothing in general, and for socks in particular. When it gets wet, it stays wet. That can lead to clammy feet. Cotton doesn't insulate when wet and it does not wick moisture, making it a poor choice in any weather.

Arm Warmers

This is another personal preference. In many instances you will warm up with arm warmers and then take them off for the race. If you do race with them on, make sure you own a pair that is tight enough that they will not slip down your arms during the race. Also, make sure you pull them up as far as possible underneath your jersey. Cyclocross incorporates your arms much more than road racing or even mountain biking. Every time you shoulder your bike it is another opportunity for your arm warmers to start migrating towards your wrists.

Knee/Leg Warmers

Knee warmers are another piece of kit that are great for warming up, but can probably be removed for most race conditions.

- Like most cold-weather gear, knee and leg warmers come in different weights. You want to find a pair that will keep you warm, but that are not so heavy that they make you overheat.
- When putting on knee warmers, first pull up your bibshorts as high as possible. Pull the knee or leg warmers up to at least mid-thigh if not a bit higher. Then cover them with your bibshorts.
- You do not want to make the mistake of not pulling the warmers up high enough. If you do, they will start to slide down your legs almost immediately and by the end of the first lap, you are going to look more like a ballet dancer than bike racer with your leg warmers around your ankles and calves. Some people even safety-pin the top of the warmer to their shorts, although this runs the risk of driving that safety-pin into your leg in the case of a fall on that side.
- If you are racing in rainy conditions, it is best to leave the knee warmers in the car or at the starting line, even if it is chilly. There is no worse feeling than riding around with soggy, heavy and cold knee warmers. It's like trying to swim with jeans on.

Vest

Vests, jackets and rain gear are items you will most likely never use in a race but still worth packing for race day. The cycling vest—or gilet—is the most versatile piece of gear when it comes to cool temperatures. Light vests usually offer wind protection in the front and a vented back. Thermal vests are insulated and offer an extra layer of protection in cold temperatures. Because it is essential to keep your core warm, a vest—in the same way a sleeveless base layer does—keeps your body warm without overheating. A cycling vest is great for wearing over a jersey on cool mornings when you are doing course review, warm-up laps or spending time on the trainer. It is also a good clothing option for the staging area. Rain pants are practically required for warming up on wet courses, as they keep your behind from getting wet, cold and miserable.

Jackets

Cycling jackets, like vests, are great for training rides and warming up for a race.

- Most cycling jackets don't breathe or regulate body temperature as efficiently as layering.
- If you are at a cold weather race, this is another piece of gear that is great to have while you wait in the staging area for your race to begin. But when the whistle blows, the jacket stays at the start line.
- Having your jacket available at the end of the race is important, too. In cold races, you will start to chill quickly after finishing and need to get warm clothing on fast.

Post-Race Wear

If you pay attention to everything in this book, you're likely to wind up on some podiums. Having a clean, dry jersey or jacket to represent your club and/or sponsor properly is good form. Likewise, one of the best parts of cyclocross is watching the races before or after your race. Make sure you've got comfortable clothes with you for doing that.

Shoes

Because cyclocross involves dismounting your bike, the shoes you wear in a race must be suitable for riding and running. Cyclocross-specific shoes don't really exist, but most mountain bike shoes will do the trick and are the choice for nearly all racers. The sport is hard on shoes and sometimes a pair worn in many muddy races may only last one season. Because you may be replacing shoes every season or buying two pairs at a time, cost should be considered when purchasing.

- When choosing a shoe, look for one that, first and foremost, is comfortable. Sure, that trendy Euro pair might turn some heads, but if they hurt your feet you're going to be dreading race day every week. Because you'll also be running in these shoes, you may want to consider sizing them slightly larger—by 1/2 a Euro size, typically—than traditional road or mountain shoes to accommodate your toes.
- Shoe choice is one of those areas in which having a relationship with a local bike store is important. Being able to try on different brands and find the shoe that works best for you is key.
- After a comfortable fit, you want a shoe that is light, has a stiff sole, and offers a tread that provides good traction.
- Most mountain bike shoes also have screw-in toe spikes that improve traction in muddy or frozen conditions. These are absolutely essential for 'cross in some conditions. A muddy or icy run-up will likely be impossible to get up without the proper toe spikes, so your shoe's ability to accept them is imperative. Bring extra spikes to races as well, sometimes a standard soccer-style spike works well (mud, sand, loose run-ups), while sometimes you'll want thin, sharp metal spikes (snow and ice). The spikes don't stay in all the time either. On a course with a set of wood or concrete stairs and no other running sections that necessitate spikes, spikes will be a detriment as it will be more awkward to run on the hard stairs.
- Because the cleats on mountain bike shoes are recessed, you will want to make sure that your pedals and cleats are compatible with the shoes you choose. Some shoes may require you to remove a little bit of tread around the cleat to enable smoother entry and exit from the pedal. You may also need to use shims to raise the cleat.
- The shoe's upper is something worth considering. A shoe with a lot of ventilation will allow more moisture to reach your feet.
- How the shoe is fastened to your foot is also worth considering. Velcro buckles will sometimes not adhere in wet and muddy conditions. Buckles and ratchets will sometimes freeze and bind during wet and cold conditions. As you become a more experienced rider, experiment with different shoes to see what works best for you.
- It's not a bad idea to have a second pair of shoes. If you are warming up on a wet or muddy course, being able to do so in your "B" shoes and then changing to your "A" shoes for the race is the best scenario. Having a second pair of shoes is also a good idea in case something goes wrong with your main pair. When the time comes to replace your race shoes, don't throw them away but rather use these as your warm up and emergency back-up shoes.
- Shoe covers (optional) are nice on cold or wet days for your warm-up. You'll almost never see riders racing in shoe covers, but it is nice to be able to keep your feet a bit warmer during pre-ride. The cheap neoprene variety is a good choice here, as it should be useful in the wet, but they will take a lot of abuse.

Helmet

The helmet doesn't need a lot of explanation. The most important thing about a helmet is to have it with you. Do not forget your helmet at home. Helmet and bike are really the only two items you must bring. Racing in your street clothes may not be the best experience but it's not against the rules. However, if you don't have a helmet—or bike—you can't race.

- If you have two helmets, bring them both. Same logic applies for helmets as it does for shoes. Having a spare means you can warm up in one and race in another. If the conditions are wet, you will have a dry helmet at the start line.
- If something breaks on your helmet, you have a spare.
- One note about helmets that cannot be stressed enough: you need to wear one at all times when riding your bike at a USA Cycling-sanctioned race. This doesn't mean just when you are on the course warming up or racing, but riding to and from your car, too. If a USA Cycling official sees you without a helmet they will most likely tell you to walk your bike. If you are a repeat offender, the officials can disqualify you from your race. They also have the authority to disqualify you from your next race if you have already finished racing that day. Finally, it is for your own safety to wear a helmet but is also to set a good example for the juniors and other kids that may be at the venue. We want them all to wear helmets and you are the role model.
- If you race in rainy weather regularly, a helmet that accepts a snap-on visor is often a nice option. While a hat with a brim under your helmet can serve the same purpose—keeping precipitation out of your eyes—a helmet visor lets you wear any hat you want.

Tights

Tights that zip up on the outside of the legs are a great piece of pre-race clothing. These tights are worn over your bibshorts or skinsuit. They are not optimal for long-distance riding but perfect for your warm up laps. When you arrive at the staging area removing these tights is a snap. Because the legs unzip, you don't have to pull the tights over your shoes. Consider ease of putting on and taking off when choosing all your warmup clothing. While a few companies make these for cycling applications, they are much more common in XC skiing. You will find a much better selection in ski shops.

Rain Jacket And Pants

Rain jacket and rain pants are other essential pieces of foul-weather gear that you will never wear in a race. If it's raining, you are going to get wet during your race. There's no avoiding it. That said, the goal is to keep as dry as possible right up until the staging of your race.

- Having a good rain jacket and rain pants allow you to recon the course and do some warm-up laps while staying warm and dry.
- Rain pants do not need to have a chamois—they are to be worn over your kit. They also double as training or commuting pants, if it rains a lot where you live. Rain pants also let you pre-ride a wet course when it's not raining, while keeping your race clothes relatively dry and clean.
- Tapered legs with elastic binders at the ankles are nice features that allow you to dismount and remount with ease during your warm-up.
- Even if you decide that the course is too muddy to do a warm-up lap (this is a consideration you need to keep in mind especially if you don't have time to clean your bike before the race or a bike wash station isn't available) having rain gear is essential for trips to registration and the porta-potty.
- We cannot stress enough the importance of showing up to the start line warm and dry. Once the race starts you will get soaked but a combination of adrenaline, race pace efforts and competitive drive should ensure that you don't feel the rain or cold until after the race has ended.

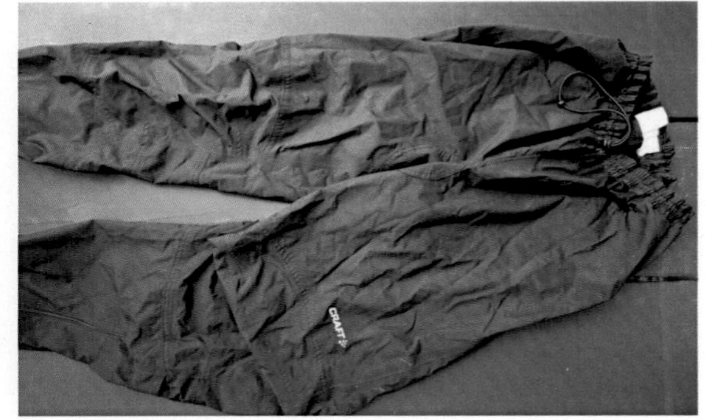

Gloves

Many pros race without gloves. This is one area in which emulating the top guys isn't the best way to go. If you race 'cross and never crash, you're a rare breed. At some point during your race season, you will hit the ground. Most likely your hands are going to be the first to hit. Your hands and fingers also risk getting roughed up while lifting the bike. There is nothing worse than cutting up your hand and not being able to ride your bike—or do just about any manual task—when something as easy as wearing gloves would have prevented the injury.

- The first choice to make is full- or half-fingered. Ultimately, it's best to have both. However, if you have only one, full-fingered gloves are the best bet. Even in warm conditions, a pair of light, well-ventilated gloves offers you the most protection. It will also take you farther into the season as conditions get colder. Once the weather gets cold, adding a second pair of gloves may be necessary.
- If it rains, glove choice becomes tricky. On a cold, rainy day, the amount of warmth protection you get from most gloves will be limited. At some point, no matter how waterproof the glove claims to be, eventually your hands are going to get wet—if not from the rain, then as the result of sweat not being able to escape. The double-edged effect of the waterproof glove is that just as water can't get in, it can't escape either. Once you start sweating, your hands will be as wet as if you had on no gloves. If sweaty hands are not an issue for you, neoprene SCUBA or fisherman-type gloves may work the best. But if you have a tendency to sweat, your best bet may be to wear a water-repellant wicking glove. The trick is to show up to the start line with a dry pair. Switch out gloves just before you race and you will have nice dry, warm hands for the first part of the race at least. By the time your hands start to get wet, you most likely will not even notice because you will be in the thick of your race and concentrating on executing your strategy. Experienced 'crossers generally bring more pairs of gloves than anything else to a race.

Caps Or Hats

A cycling cap in many instances is a personal preference. Some people like the aesthetic or comfort of the cap.

- The bill offers some shading from the sun and in rainy weather keeps some water out of your eyes. However, it can also require you to hold your head at a higher angle to look ahead when racing in the drops, in a low position. As with all equipment choices, experiment in training before using something at a race.

- In cold weather, a cap can hold in warmth. But make sure you don't overheat. Because a significant amount of your body heat escapes through the head, if it is a warm day, you are going to overheat.
- If you are racing in really cold weather, covering your ears with a headband, thin skullcap or cap with earflaps will keep you dry and comfortable.
- Make sure you have done a hard 45-minute effort in a cap in training to make sure it's comfortable. Unlike gloves or arm warmers that can be easily discarded, once a cap is on, it's staying on for the entire race.

Eyewear

- Sunglasses are not a necessity in 'cross races.
- If it is a dry, dusty course, sunglasses will add a level of protection.
- For overcast days, having clear lenses is a great option.
- In rainy or muddy conditions, be aware that your glasses may get splattered at some point during the race. If this happens, be prepared to remove your glasses. If you have a friend or teammate watching the race hand off the frames to them as you ride by.
- You can also toss them into the pits or somewhere outside the tape. If you do this, make sure you remember to go back and pick up the frames after the race. On average, two to three pairs of high-end sunglasses end up in the promoter's lost and found box every race weekend.

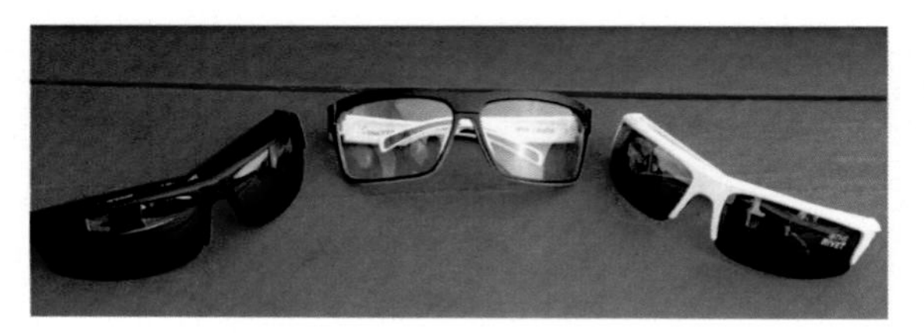

Embrocation

The decision to ditch the knee warmers goes hand-in-hand with another topic that can be a bit exotic and mysterious to the new racer: embrocation. This thick, creamy substance that many cold-weather cyclists rub on their legs for warmth and protection against the rain has found a place in the modern culture of cyclocross. Do you need to apply embrocation to race 'cross? No. Is it going to make you faster? Doubtful. Will it offer some level of comfort? It could. Try it out and see for yourself. Cold weather embrocation contains ingredients such as chili pepper extract that create a warming sensation. It is activated by moisture, so when you start sweating or when the rain comes, the embrocation kicks in.

In wet and cold conditions, the protective and warming properties of embrocation may do more to keep you comfortable than knee or leg warmers. Now, you may be saying to yourself, why am I being told not to wear leg or knee warmers to race in cold temperatures when every training article ever written is emphatic that knees must be covered if the riding temperature is below 70°? This is good advice. The difference, however, is that the 70° rule applies to long training rides that last for several hours. By contrast, cyclocross races only last from 30 minutes to an hour.

If you warm up properly, stay covered, keep dry before the start and use embrocation, exposure to cold temperatures for this relatively short period of time will not be detrimental. That being said, if having your legs exposed in cold weather races is going to detract from your performance, by all means, wear knee or leg warmers.

EMBROCATION APPLICATION

Anyone who has used embrocation for the first time may have learned the hard way that, whatever you do, keep embrocation away from the body parts where you don't want a burning sensation—namely your eyes and your chamois area.

- **Before applying the hot stuff on your legs, keep this mantra in mind: "bibs before embro."**
- **Always pull on your bib shorts or skinsuit before applying the embrocation.**
- **You can easily roll up the legs of your bibs and apply the embro to your upper legs, but if you apply the embro first, you run the risk of your chamois rubbing against your leg and picking up excess embrocation as you pull on your bibs. This is a disaster waiting to happen.**

- Embrocation can be applied with wax paper or a towel dedicated to that purpose. You can also use your fingers, but always remember to wipe down your hands with rubbing alcohol or witch hazel after doing so. Plastic or latex gloves work well for this too.
- Dedicate a second towel to the clean up process.
- When you are done racing, use the rubbing alcohol or witch hazel—baby wipes with rubbing alcohol work great for this purpose—to remove embrocation from your legs and anywhere else you applied it.
- Soap and water alone do not remove embrocation. This becomes crystal clear the first time you shower after applying embrocation. Many people have the shared experience of not thinking embrocation did anything until they showered and their legs felt like they were on fire.

Chamois Cream

Embrocation might be optional, but chamois cream is generally not. Many people develop sores or abrasions in the saddle area if they don't apply some sort of cream or ointment to reduce friction. Experiment with different brands and styles to see what works for you. Chamois cream should be in every racer's gear bag.

Ziplock Freezer Bags

Large freezer bags are perfect for storing items in your gear bag. If you have multiple sets of gloves, put them all in a freezer bag. Same with socks, caps, kits, etc. This is a great way to organize your gear so that you aren't frantically searching for that missing sock instead of reconnoitering the course.

Plastic shopping bags or garbage bags are great for piles of wet gear after the race and take up minimal space.

Water Bottles

- Bring at least three to the race.
- Fill your bottles with water before leaving home because you can't be sure that water will be provided at the race venue.
- You should have one bottle for when you are warming-up, one bottle to take with you to staging and one bottle for post-race.
- You do not need to have a bottle during the race. In fact, your bike shouldn't include bottle cages because they interfere with carrying the bike.

- For your pre-race bottles, adding a drink mix solution that includes carbohydrates and electrolytes is a good idea. There are many of these products on the market. It is worth trying out several to see what works best for you. Drink mixes affect people differently. You want to make sure you choose one for race day that is not going to upset your stomach.
- Your post-race bottle should contain a drink designed to speed recovery. That generally means some carbohydrates, but also a bit of protein. This can be a commercial recovery drink, a fruit and protein smoothie you blended at home or something as simple as chocolate milk.

PACKING SUMMARY

- Jerseys (short sleeve, long sleeve)
- Bibshorts
- Skinsuit (optional)
- Base Layers (light, medium, heavy)
- Socks (thick wool, thin synthetic)
- Arm Warmers (optional for warm ups)
- Leg Warmers (optional for warm ups)
- Knee Warmers (optional for warm ups)
- Tights (optional, also good for staging)
- Vest (optional for warm ups)
- Winter Jacket
- Rain Jacket/Pants (optional for warm ups)
- Shoes
- Helmet
- Gloves
- Cap/Hat
- Sunglasses (optional)
- Embrocation (optional)
- Chamois cream
- Water bottles (x3)
- Plastic bags (garbage/grocery and ziplock freezer)

THE TOOLBOX

At many larger races, there will be a neutral-support mechanic, usually a local bike store that has volunteered to set up an area for fixing small mechanical mishaps. However, it is never a good idea to assume a mechanic is going to be on site. Along with learning how to prepare yourself to race, it is equally important that you learn how to prepare your bike for racing. This means knowing how to do basic maintenance from changing a flat and switching cassettes to adjusting brakes and derailleurs. It's not a bad idea to purchase a small toolbox. It does not have to be fancy or expensive. A cheap plastic box from your hardware store will do the trick. You may never use all of the tools in your toolbox, but it is good to be prepared for that one time when you need the tool on the bottom of your box. It is also good to be the person that always has the tool somebody else needs. It is a great way to make friends in the racing community.

Allen Wrenches

Allen wrenches are essential tools for bike maintenance. Adjusting your handlebars, saddle, fork and derailleurs can all be accomplished with a set of Allen wrenches. A multi-tool will work fine, but you might want to purchase a "Y" wrench or two. These usually come as a 2mm, 2.5mm and 3mm Allen wrench combo, and a 4mm, 5mm and 6mm Allen wrench combo. If you are running a brand of cantilever brakes with cartridge pads, you will also need a smaller wrench, usually 1mm or 1.5mm to loosen the retainer screw. Also make sure you know how to install your pedals. Most modern pedals use an Allen wrench rather than a pedal wrench for installation and this wrench can be as large as 8mm. If so, this is another size you should have in your toolbox. An 8mm wrench is used to install many brands of cranks. Having this size wrench available is never a bad idea, especially if you discover your cranks are loose before your race begins.

Spoke Wrenches

Spoke wrenches come in several sizes. Make sure you know which size spoke nipple your wheels use and have a spoke wrench that works on your wheel. For wheels with bladed spokes you also need a separate tool—or you can use your needle nose pliers—to secure the spoke you are adjusting so that it doesn't twist.

Sometimes at a race, a wheel can go out of true, which is when your rim wobbles while spinning. If you are doing your recon lap, or just riding around, and you hit a root, rock, curb or a barrier that knocks your wheel out of true, you are going to need a spoke wrench to get it spinning smoothly. If your wheel is a little out of true, don't worry about it. But if the rim is rubbing against the brake pad in a spot, and you have a couple minutes to fix it, do so. Set your bike in a workstand, hang it on a car rack (not a roof rack) or turn the bike upside down like you did as a kid. Slowly spin the offending wheel until the rim rubs against the brake pad. Locate the spoke closest to the rub that is attached to the hub on the opposite side as the rub. Tighten that spoke a quarter turn. When using a spoke wrench, tightening and loosening are opposite of what a screwdriver does. After tightening that spoke, loosen the spokes near the rub that attach to the hub on the same side as the rub by a quarter turn. Spin the wheel. If the pad and rim still make contact repeat the tightening and loosening routine until the rim has moved far enough back to center. After your race, make sure to check the rim again and have it trued on a truing stand if necessary.

Cassette Tools

Cassette tools are used to remove a cassette from the wheel hub. The cassette tool comes in to play if your cassette malfunctions or in the rare instances in which you pre-ride a course and believe you need a different gear combination. To remove a cassette, you will also need a chain whip and an adjustable wrench. Place the cassette tool into the lock ring of the cassette, which is located in the center of the cassette. The tool is splined and should slot into the lock ring easily. The chain whip is placed on a cog of the cassette to stop it from spinning while you loosen the lock ring. The adjustable wrench, or a second chain whip (if it has a wrench end on the handle) is placed on the cassette tool and used to turn the tool and loosen the lock ring. Once loosened, the lock ring and cassette cogs can be removed and replaced with a different cassette. Once that is in place, put the cassette tool back on the cassette and use the adjustable wrench or wrench end of a chain whip to tighten the lock ring. You do not need to use a chain whip on the cassette cogs to tighten the lock ring, only to loosen it. Including an extra cassette lock ring—and Shimano cassette spacer, if you are using Shimano cassettes—is a good idea, but not absolutely necessary.

Needle-Nose Pliers

Needle-nose pliers come in handy for cinching cable-ends onto the ends of cables. This is a good general-purpose tool to have around that you won't know you need until you need it.

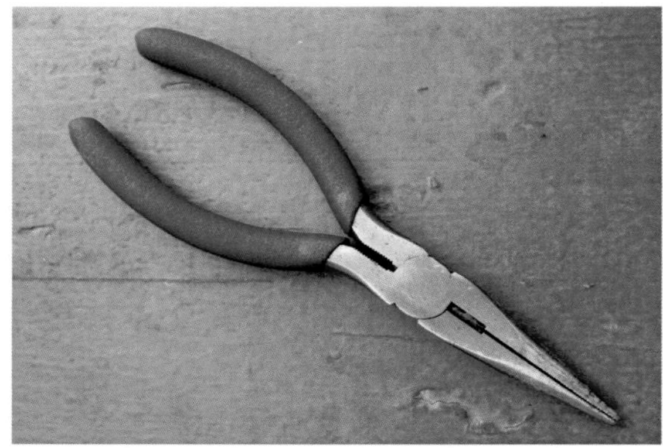

Cable Cutter

A cable cutter is a tool used to cut brake or shifter cables. At some point during your racing career, you will snap a cable and need to replace it. This is a repair that takes several minutes to complete and one that should not be attempted for the first time before you are about to race. Your best bet is to go to the neutral support mechanic to see if they can repair the broken cable. The other route to take is to start re-cabling your own bikes now, so that when this happens on race day you have the skills necessary to do the repair on your own. It should go without saying that to replace brake or shifter cables you need to pack spares in your toolbox. You also should keep spare housing in the box. Keep in mind that brake and shifter cables are not interchangeable. Brake cables are thicker and have different ends than shifter cables. If replacing cables isn't yet in your comfort zone, you can still use the cable cutters to quickly repair frayed cables. Then use your needle-nose pliers to fasten the ferrule to the cable. Applying a new ferrule is great if you have time, but not a necessary repair if you are running short on time.

Screwdriver

A screwdriver is necessary to adjust the limiter screws on your derailleur. Make sure ahead of time that you have an appropriately-sized screwdriver for your limiter screws. Usually, these screws accept both Phillips and flat head screwdrivers. You need a screwdriver with a thin enough head to fit into the limiter screw. Test out screwdrivers ahead of race day to ensure they work for your derailleurs. Place one of each type in your tool box. Familiarize yourself ahead of race day where the limiter screws are on your derailluers. There is a high and low limiter screw on each. The high limiter screw on the front derailleur is usually the outside screw and is sometimes marked with an H. Adjust this screw if your chain is falling off to the outside of the big chain ring when you shift from small to the big chainring or if the chain is having difficulty shifting from the small ring to the big ring. The low limiter screw on the front derailleur is usually the screw closest to the frame and will sometimes be denoted by an L. Adjust the low limiter screw if the chain falls off the chainring to the inside of the small chainring when shifted from big to small. For adjustments to either screw, start with a quarter turn and try shifting. Repeat until the chain stays on the rings and shifts smoothly.

Zip Ties

Zip ties can be used for on-the-fly repairs such as attaching cable housing to a frame, if a braze-on fails. They are also good to have around if you are entered in a race that requires bike numbers. If you have a catastrophic mechanical, such as a rear derailleur that snaps, zip ties are good for securing the parts to the frame until you can get the bike home or to the shop.

Wrenches

An assortment of wrenches in sizes such as 9, 10 and 11mm will come in handy for making adjustments to cantilever brakes. Minor brake adjustments are not uncommon on race day. If your brakes are squealing, toe in the brake pads. Try using a credit card or hotel room key placed between the rim and the rear of the brake pad to create a slight inward angle of the brake pad while adjusting it. The brakes from above will look as if they are pigeon-toed. Thus the "toed-in" moniker.

Electrical Tape

Electrical tape is your best bet for fixing handlebar tape. In a pinch it can be used not only to reattach the handlebar tape at the ends, but to fix tape that has torn somewhere in the middle. If you crash during your warm-up lap, the handlebar tape may come loose. Being able to quickly refasten it is why you have the electrical tape. For last-minute repairs, your main concern is functionality not style.

Rag And Chain Lubrication

A bottle of chain lubrication and a rag to wipe down your chain after lubrication should also take up permanent residence in your toolbox.

Spare Parts

It is a good idea to keep some spare parts in your toolbox. These include extra skewers for your wheels. Make sure you have a front and rear skewer. Also, have a spare seatpost binder bolt, stem bolts, brake pads, ferrules for your cable ends, spare shifter and brake cables and housing, Shimano cassette spacer and handlebar tape. For those running deep-rimmed wheels, spare valve extenders are a must. If you are racing a single-speed bike, having a few different sized cogs is always a good idea. You may find your gearing is a bit too steep after a warm-up lap and want to swap it out for a larger, easier gearing option. Also, it is a good practice to have spare tubular tires and tire adhesive, if you are away for more than a single day of racing.

Bottle Opener

A bottle opener is always a useful tool to keep in your box. Even if you don't drink, many folks at races do and if you are the only one with the opener, everybody will love you.

Extra Tubes

If you are running clinchers for your race, always bring extra tubes. Three is a safe number. Keep one at the bottom of your gear bag and two in your toolbox so even if you forget the box, you still have the tube.

Chain Tool, Spare Chain And Quick Link

A chain tool, spare chain and quick link are essential items for your toolkit. You may go seasons without breaking a chain at a race, but when it happens you want to make sure you have the necessary tools and parts to make the repair. It is a personal preference whether you want to replace or fix a chain. As a general rule, you should replace a chain every 3,000 miles. If you have a lot of miles on the chain, replacing may be your best option. However, if you are strapped for time, removing the broken link and reattaching the chain may be your best bet. Regardless, it is advisable to replace the chain soon after your race.

DIY CHAIN TOOL

A good trick for refastening a chain is to get a metal dry cleaner hanger and cut a straight four- or five-inch section. Bend the hanger about an inch from each end so that it resembles a C with sharp corners. Place the hanger piece into the third or fourth link from the broken ends of the chain. This will create slack in the chain and make attaching the ends easier.

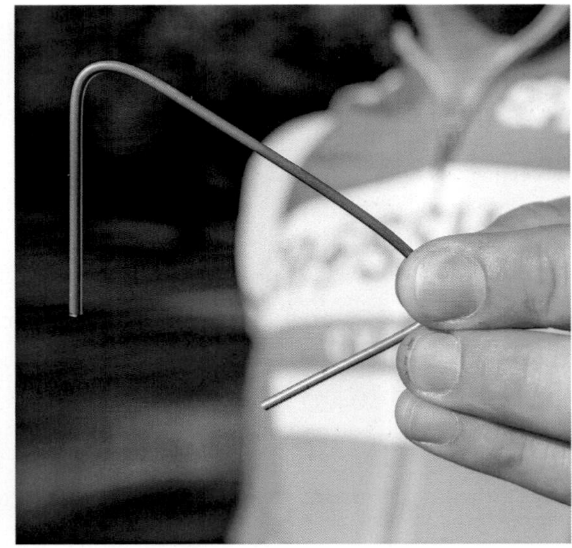

Cleaning Bucket

A cleaning bucket with a bottle of dishwashing soap and brushes in it should be a part of your race-day gear. Also, bring a container—an empty one-gallon milk jug would work—filled with water in case there is no hose available at the venue. If the course is muddy, you will want to wash down your drivetrain after a practice lap. Your pit helper may also need to wash down your bike between laps, if you are running two bikes and the race is muddy.

Plastic Trash Bags And Towels

Plastic trash bags and towels are two essential items to bring to any race but will be crucial on muddy days. When you finish racing on a wet or muddy day, you should go back to your vehicle and change out of your wet kit. Being able to change clothes efficiently while having a bath towel wrapped around your waist is a skill you will master in no time, as you begin disrobing in parking lots on a regular basis. You will also find that your comfort-level with walking around half-naked in public spaces will increase significantly the more you start to race. From skintight kits to parking lot nakedness, bike racing is not and will never be a bastion of modesty. Once you have removed your wet kit, socks, gloves and anything else you had on to race, put all of it into a plastic trash bag. Your shoes can go in a separate bag. Change clothes, put on rain gear, if necessary, and find the bike wash. Hose down your bike (this should take no more than three minutes if done properly) and towel it dry with clean rags. Place the rags in the plastic bag with your kit, or in their own bag. Having all of your muddy gear in plastic bags keeps your car mud-free and makes washing everything once you get home much easier. If your kit is full of mud, your best bet when you get home is to lay out your gear in the yard, driveway or patio and hose it all down before throwing everything into the washing machine. This will make the actual cleaning job significantly easier and reduce the wear and tear on your appliances.

First Aid Kit

Keep band-aids, bandages, gauze, tape and antibiotic ointment in your gear bag or tool kit. If you never need any of these items, you're not racing hard enough.

Tire Pump and Accurate, Consistent Pressure Gauge

A floor pump that has a pressure gauge is an invaluable tool. Floor pumps offer the most ease of use. If you want that pro touch, use a battery-powered inflator like the one shown at right. Even more important than the gauge being accurate is that it is consistent. Once you know what pressure works for you on that particular pump, you will always be able to dial in your preferred pressure.

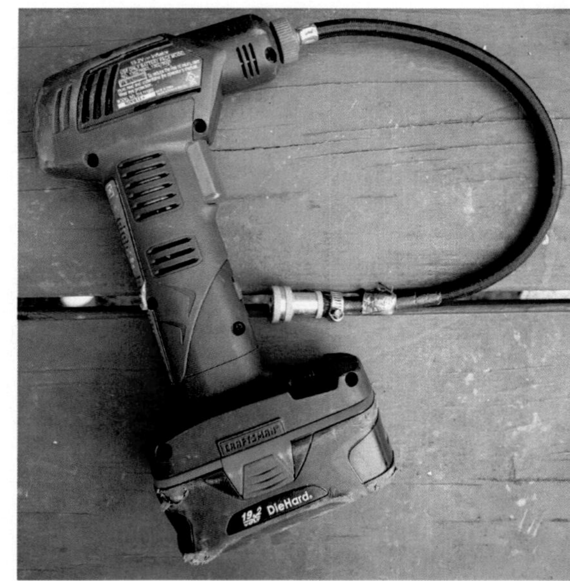

Rapha